The
Joy of
MUSIC MINISTRY

The Joy of MUSIC MINISTRY

John Michael Talbot

Resurrection Press
An Imprint of
CATHOLIC BOOK PUBLISHING CO.
Totowa • New Jersey

Dedicated to the memory of
Yvonne Perkins

First published in September, 2001 by Resurrection Press, Catholic Book Publishing Company.

Copyright © 2001 by John Michael Talbot

ISBN 1-878718-63-0

Library of Congress Catalog Number: 01-132737

Cover design by John Murello

Cover photo © Howard DeCruyenaere, 2000

Printed in Canada.

1 2 3 4 5 6 7 8 9

Contents

Foreword... 7

Introduction..10

Chapter 1: The Music of God 14

Chapter 2: Biblical Basics..43

Chapter 3: Church Teaching...71

Chapter 4: The Master Musician.................................. 87

Foreword

IT'S always dangerous to read a book on an airplane. I've laughed and cried as flight attendants have asked if there was anything they could do to make my flight more enjoyable. As I read the script for John Michael's new book on music ministry, I wanted to jump up and shout out, "He gets it." I am not sure the other passengers would have appreciated my enthusiasm at 35,000 feet. But I do believe that if we could take to heart John Michael's insights, these fellow passengers (pilgrims) would cheer with me at their next Sunday Mass.

I am not a musician; I am a liturgist and a pastor. In my liturgical studies I came to understand that the liturgy and music of the Church belong to all of us. Even those of us who cannot sing or play an instrument have a right to full participation in the worship of God. The gifted ones are asked to use their talents to call the best out of us, to allow us to enter the mystery of the liturgy, and to make us look and sound better than we really are. If that is not enough of a challenge, the true minister actually inspires us to believe we can use MUSIC to praise and worship the living God. I admit, the challenge is huge.

I first started to be involved with liturgical music back in the late 70s. I became a liturgical consultant for a great music company called North American Liturgical Resources (NALR). I was blessed to be involved with the formation and distribution of the *Glory and Praise* Songbooks. I saw the enthusiasm this new kind of music was bringing. I also witnessed the tension. Some people felt as if the Church were selling out its tradition of music as art. In our hearts, however, we knew that it was a unique time and that the Church was re-capturing its own tradition of full, conscious, and active participation in the Mass.

It was at this time I met John Michael. It was clear he had the voice of the angels and that he was a musician of outstanding talent. Little did we know that soon after his conversion to the Catholic family, he would end up a prophet, speaking for God and calling the Church toward renewal. In everything he would do, he would push himself beyond what was expected and by his example he would call the rest of us to go beyond our ordinary lives.

The Joy of Music Ministry goes beyond expectations, as well. JMT develops a theology of the Christian life, an understanding of Church, a fresh view of the liturgy, and a deeper look at the power of music in the spiritual life. He understands music as a tool that God uses to communicate and a tool the Church uses to form and transform its people. He "gets it" that music *evokes* a response and has a power in the human soul that often goes beyond words. JMT realizes we are at a special time and with the proper use of technology and new styles of music we can evangelize in new ways. For all of these insights, I am grateful.

A few weeks ago I had a rap session with 400 high school teens from our parish LIFE TEEN program. I asked the teens to tell me about themselves. "What are you guys into these days? Sports? The Internet?" Over 90% of the teens present said "Music." "What kind of music?" I asked. The answer was pretty clear it wasn't a particular style of music, it was just music.

Why can't we use music—their music, your music, my music— to worship God? We CAN. With special care for the dignity of the liturgy, we find that the Catholic (universal) Church is big enough to include other cultures, other styles, and other tastes in the way we praise God.

I encourage every pastor, musician, parish staff member, and anyone interested in the renewal of the Church to read this book. All who read it will walk away with a deeper understanding of the priority of the liturgy, the importance of music, and the loving acceptance of God.

I have believed for years the true renewal of the Roman Catholic Church would come when we found a way to combine three things: 1) orthodox Catholic teaching 2) priority of our liturgical tradition 3) spirit-filled praise and worship. For me John Michael captures these beliefs and gives biblical and Church documentation to further our understanding. He clearly sees that God can use the music minister as an instrument of renewal. That's why music ministers can approach their craft with a deep sense of joy.

For twenty-five years John Michael Talbot has been blessing the Church with his music and his teachings. Today, with this book and with his insights into music ministry, John Michael serves the Church in a new and powerful way.

—Fr. Dale Fushek
Vicar General, Diocese of Phoenix
Founder, LIFE TEEN Program

Introduction

ST. Augustine said, "he who sings, prays twice." It is said that, "Bach gave us God's word, Mozart gave us God's laughter, and Beethoven gave us God's fire. God gave us music that we might pray without words." Among all of the arts the Church has esteemed music highest among the others.

Music is sacramental. It symbolizes spirituality already present, and causes that spirituality to grow stronger. In the theological language of the sacraments it, "symbolizes, and effects grace." It is said that a kiss is sacramental for it symbolizes the love that exists already, yet causes that love to grow stronger. While a kiss does not constitute the fullness of the sacrament of matrimony, it most appropriately is part of it. Like a kiss between lovers in the sacrament of matrimony, music can be sacramental in the special liturgies of the seven formal sacraments.

This work is titled *The Joy of Music Ministry*. As a Catholic Christian music minister I am tempted to respond, "say what?" Yes, music ministers are frequently a very melancholy bunch. We can be moody! We often feel misunderstood, used, and abused, especially when working in a supportive role, such as in liturgy or for various ceremonies. Both those in authority and the congregation or participants in such functions are less than concert quality listeners. But I have found that serving in such a capacity is good for my

Christian faith, which calls me to serve rather than to be served, to notice others rather than seeking to be noticed.

It is this melancholy temperament that also makes musicians and many other artists, excellent vehicles for the more intuitive aspects of a relationship with God. We can pick up on the Word that is beyond words, the meaning proclaimed in the emotion behind a note, or the word proclaimed in the silence between the notes. Potentially in rebirth through Christ, this takes the musician beyond a mere temperamental artist to the spiritual realms of a true mystic.

The Joy of Music Ministry will take us on a journey in Christ and the Church. We will begin with an understanding of what the mystics call the Music of God. This will include the mystical teaching that God created all of creation through music. But this is not just music you can hear with your ears. It is the music of the harmony and peace of God. It is found in the Trinity and freely overflows into all creation. When creation is subjected to discord through humanity's choice to try and make music without God, or what we call sin, God reaches out through Jesus to restore the original Music of God in the human family and throughout all creation. This call is personal to each of us in the call to discipleship and demands our personal response. Since we then find others who have also decided to follow Jesus, this response is corporate as well. This implies the reality of the Church, the Word, and

Sacrament. We will then look at the use of music during the summit of our corporate experience as gathered Christians, the Eucharist. We will simply walk through a typical liturgy and see the potential for spiritual music in each part of the Mass and how the music we hear can aid everyone in participating more fully in Christ and the Church.

In Chapter 2 we will look at the scriptural basis of the use of music. We might be a little surprised by how much music is really involved in God's work on earth! Music is used for worship, as most of us know from its use during liturgy and other Church services. But it is also used in the ministry of the prophets and the teachers of the Church. It is used to stir up the various charismatic gifts, such as healing and deliverance from evil spirits and negative moods. Contemporary experience also teaches us that it can be used in evangelization, using the music of a culture to reach the people of that culture with the gospel of Jesus Christ.

After this we will look at the documents of the Church containing the primary teachings of the Magesterium from the last century. I will not quote them extensively, but rather will summarize their contents in a way that is relevant to the issues we face today. We will see how they affect the style, training, and spirituality of the sacred musician's ministry in liturgical and paraliturgical settings.

From here we will conclude with the Master Musician teaching I have given in the past that includes a more complete look at the various musical styles and the configuration of players used to make them, and how they correspond to the various aspects of life in the Church. This ranges all the way from the rock and jazz band, to the full-blown symphony orchestra, to the use of the soloist in them all. They all correspond to life in the Church, and teach all of us much about expanding our horizons when participating in the Church as Catholic Christians.

So let us begin the journey. I pray that this little book will be used in a powerful way to help you hear and participate in making the music of God in the Church and in God's wonderful world. May discord be brought back into the harmony of God. May division be brought back into unity in diversity. And may the error of hatred be brought back into the love and truth of God, through Jesus Christ our Lord. Amen.

Chapter 1

The Music of God

BEFORE we look at some specific applications of music ministry in scripture and liturgy, let's look at the whole analogy of music for the Catholic Christian life. Before we can engage in the specific ministry of music, we must first have some grasp of the Music of God in the Symphony Orchestra of the Church and the world. The following is found in greater length and theological completeness in my previous works, *Music of Creation*, and *The Master Musician*, but I hope that this shorter treatment will still be helpful here.

Creation

You may think that music can only be heard by the ear or perceived by other sense organs. But music can be heard in the spirit and the soul as well. Many mystics say that God created all creation with music, for He is music itself. But this spiritual music is much deeper than the kind we think of in our world today.

The music of the spirit has to do with perfect balance and harmony in all things. It is the perfect proportion of rhythm and harmony, that originally flowed through all things, not the least of which was the human being. It is still there to some degree. Once we find it for ourselves, we see it in all else as well. All is created anew.

Sound is nothing more than waves of energy perceived primarily, but not exclusively, through the ears. Music is the harmonious proportion and rhythm of these energy waves. These waves of energy are also in what we see through light waves and in what we touch, taste, and feel through the other sensory perceptions. Even solid objects are made up of molecules that pulsate at different speeds to form various materials. All creation is only a wave of energy perceived more clearly for human beings through the different sensory perceptions.

It is said that insects and reptiles have other sense organs or different use of the ones they share with humans. Thus, an insect such as the bee might be able to see a different spectrum of light than what we can see and the pit viper is able to sense movement and temperature with the pits around its mouth.

Some mystics are said to have had visions of heaven whereby they say that color is "heard" like music, and sound is "seen" like a color. They say that in heaven normal things take on a whole new shimmer and shine that is nothing short of miraculous! Perhaps this is why the Book of Revelation says that in heaven there are streets, "like transparent gold," or why Jesus' resurrected body could appear in a room without coming through the door, or take on the appearance of a stranger. No doubt, the spiritual reality God originally planned for creation is all based on being able to fully perceive this "music" in all things. Once we learn of this music, all things begin to sing!

Part of making this music is having our human person in proper order, or peace. Using the anthropology of St. Paul, we can define the human being as having a spirit, soul, and body. Due to our current condition we usually think of these things the other way around, or body, soul, spirit. Body is our senses and emotions. Soul is the spiritual mind, or the ability to be cognitively aware of reality. Body and soul are the house of the spirit and are rightly engaged in the things of space and time. Spirit is the deepest reality of our being. It is pure spiritual intuition that is beyond senses, emotions, or thoughts, but builds on, complements, and completes them all. In union with God's Spirit, our spirit has a wonderful and unique capacity for eternity and infinity. It is present in eternity in the now and does all things even while body and soul are engaged in the matters of space and time.

The Eastern Christian fathers say that body and soul constitute the energies of the human being. Spirit constitutes essence. Energies are perceptible and knowable through sense, emotion, or thought.

Essence is perceptible only through spiritual intuition. As the mystics say, this can only be "known through unknowing." All of creation is also made of energies and essence. God, too, has uncreated energies and essence. Energies can be perceived and known through sense, emotion, and thought. Essence can only be known through spiritual intuition, or contemplation.

Learning how to progress from perceiving energies to perceiving this essence in God and all of creation, opens us up to a whole new reality. It is a whole new way of seeing everything. When the spirit is first in our priorities of human function, then we can tune into the original pulsating rhythms and proportions of God's energies and essence in everything, most especially in the human being and the Church. It is learning how to hear God's music in and through all that is.

This reordering is called many things by the different world religions. Some Hindus and Buddhists call it Kensho, or Samadhi. In English we usually hear it called breakthrough, awakening, or rebirth. Contemporary Christians, using biblical language, call it being born again. In Catholic Christianity, among other things, we call it conversion, or rebirth in the Spirit of Christ. The mystics say it is fully experienced in the state of contemplation. But we are getting ahead of ourselves a bit.

When the spirit is the primary and leading faculty of the human being, then all the rest fall into harmony, peace, and right order. The mind serves the things of spirit, so thoughts are clear and focused. The emotions are directed by the spirit, so they become the proper empowerment and motivator of the spiritual life. The senses become the strong and efficient house, or vehicle, for this wonderful harmony of being called humanity, so the body becomes natural, healthy and whole.

In this original state of being, humankind reflected the Music of the Creator and helped continue the Song on earth. While body and soul walked the things of space and time in perfect order, the spirit expanded throughout all eternity and infinity. Without losing full presence to the here and now, the spirit became intuitively present everywhere in a state of being that was fully awake and alive. It was a music that could be heard, not only with ears and other sense organs, but also with the whole Being in God. In this music, all of creation was joined together without losing the integrity or beauty of any individual thing to make a music that permeated all in all. It was the Music of God.

The Fall

When these aspects of our humanity get turned around, we get into the terrible mess we see throughout creation today. "The Fall," or the effects of original sin have intimate and personal causes and ramifications that hit very close to home, right here in our comfortable, western world.

It starts in the way we function with the basic body, soul, and spirit "stuff" of which we are made. When the senses of the body lead the way, we become primarily concerned with sense gratification. Rather than being positively incarnational, we become "sensual" or "carnal." This can be negative. It can affect the other areas of our being as well. When we don't get what we want, we become angry and upset. When the emotions become clouded, the thoughts become conflicted, unfocused, and confused. The spirit gets totally ignored and covered up in this chaotic cacophony of discord. It is as if the spirit is asleep, or even dead. The spirit has to be reborn in order to turn things back around, or to go through conversion. The spirit has to be awakened.

This is the typical mode of existence for most of humanity today. Despite our many leaps forward through science and technology, humanity remains deeply trapped in the things that have imprisoned us throughout our time on this planet. Never before in history has so much good been possible and so much evil been done. Never before have there been so many wars on the face of the earth at one time. Never before have so many civilians been tortured and slaughtered. Never before have so many children been destroyed through abortion, hunger, and war. While we now have the ability to educate, provide medical care, employ, and feed the whole world, most of the world goes to bed hungry, sick, and without proper education, medical care, or employment. Despite our progress, we have not really solved much at all. Despite our development of external music and the arts, we remain deep in sleep within a tomb of carnality and self-centeredness that impede us from singing and playing the music we have been created to make.

Today we are trapped in the constant cycle of suffering, of birth and death that are orchestrated to the discordant cries of the rule of the flesh. The big things start with the small. "I'm hot, I'm cold, I'm tired, I'm hungry," are the cries that still rise up from the most temporally blessed civilization to have ever existed on the face of the earth. Tragically, these cries of carnal selfishness often drown out the cries of real poverty, injustice, and war.

The emotions are disturbed by the tyranny of the senses. When we do not get the sense gratification we want, we get upset. Anger, lust, jealousy, and all the other unruly emotions associated with our unnatural lifestyle of anxiety, tension, and stress, trouble most people today. Road rage is the emotion of the new urban warrior. Computer temper tantrums have surprised almost anyone who has plugged into the new information highway. Anger is the number one concern of many of those who come to our Retreat Center. Most of us are troubled by unruly emotions that seem to control our life, instead of using them to empower our life for the better.

When the emotions are unruly and out of control, the thoughts of the mind become unfocused, cloudy, and confused. Most of us are unable to enter into meditation for even a short period of time without getting seriously distracted. Distractions have always been an issue in classical meditation, but today it is far more exaggerated. When this occurs, it is difficult to discern the will of God for the more obvious, objective areas of our life, much less the deeper, mystical areas of spirit and soul. Most of us are disturbed by negative thoughts and fantasies that go contrary to what we really believe to be the morally and spiritually best thing for our life.

When this is the state of the human being, even religion can remain something external to the essence of our being. Yes, we may believe all the right things about doctrine, sacraments, and ecclesiology. We may spend hours at our devotions, bible studies, rosaries, novenas, intercessions, and adoration. But religion and God remain something extrinsic to our deepest being. They remain on the outside. Ironically, I have seen people spend hours and sometimes days in Eucharistic adoration and still miss the very Jesus who is present in that same Eucharist! We may read vast volumes about meditation, contemplation, and mystical prayer or spend thousands of hours in meditation. All of these things are good in and of themselves. They are legitimate tools from God. But all of these things can remain extrinsic, or outside of our deepest being and essence.

Believe me, as Spiritual Father of The Brothers and Sisters of Charity at Little Portion Hermitage, I have seen many young monks get stuck in this tragic place. Despite all of our efforts in prayer and the like, we often remain "on the outside looking in," because we have inadvertently left God on the outside of our very being. We do this by continuing to functionally operate with the senses and emotions of the body, or even the thoughts of the mind or soul, before the things of the spirit. Only when we place the spirit first do the other things come together in a way that becomes the Music of God.

All the various teachings of the religions of the world on meditation or contemplation take us through a journey to reorder these aspects of our humanity so we might have peace. We call them different things in different Christian and non-Christian traditions, but all attempt to do the same thing—to reorder the senses of the body. Then we work on the thoughts and emotions. Only then does the spirit awaken in a rebirth that leads us from slavery to a false self to the freedom of the truth.

The Christian West would lead us through sacred reading or *lectio divina*, meditation, and contemplation. Later mystics in the West would also speak of the purgative, illuminative, and unitive ways. The Christian East would lead us from the Incensive Power, to the Rational Power, to Intellection, or spiritual intuition. The Taoists would work on Vitality, Energy, and Essence, corresponding to our western descriptions of body, soul, and spirit.

The following chart might be helpful in visualizing these sets of threes:

West/East	Far East	East	Early West	Later West
Body	Body/Vitality	Incensive	Reading	Purgative
Soul	Mind/Energy	Rational	Meditation	Illuminative
Spirit	Spirit/Essence	Intellection	Contemplation	Unitive

Redemption/Incarnation

The good news is that creation bears God's traces and humanity bears God's image, so despite our discordant inversion of God's harmony, we still seek the things of God. Humanity seeks truth, goodness, beauty, justice, and love. Human beings are also innately religious. We seek the things of the spirit and things eternal, even from the midst of the impermanence of the created order. Whenever we seek these things, we are seeking God from within.

The Catholic Church teaches that whatever is good and true in any other philosophy or religion, ultimately comes from God. Religion represents the best longings of humanity for God. Religion is humanity reaching out for God. Often we find part, or even much, of the fullness of God in that inspiration to reach out for things spiritual and Divine. So we see a longing for the original Music of God in all the religions of the world, and to a greater or lesser degree, a sharing in the restoration of the Divine Song. The Church would teach that much of this can be used by the Catholic Christian as long as it is first "baptized," as it were, in Christ. This is true especially in the area of meditation and the cooperative work among the religions to help build a better and more just world.

Then something wonderful happened. God reached back! Yes, He was always there in His Spirit in creation and humanity, but this was something different. In a most unique and wonderful way God reached back to, and through, the people of Israel to manifest something beyond what we could find on our own through creation and humanity. This is called "Revelation."

In the Old Testament we believe God began His Revelation through the law and the prophets. He raised up patriarchs and prophets like Moses. He led the Jews from bondage to freedom. Then He gave us the law. It is as if He sent humanity a letter through His especially chosen people, who were to be His messengers. He sent us a letter preparing humanity for a personal visit, an Incarnation. The letter was wonderful. It told us much about Himself, where humanity comes from and where we are going. It helped us with many of the mundane details of being a people dedicated to the things of His Spirit.

Yet something was still missing. It was as if God had sent us the score to the symphony and even a recording to get an idea of what it sounds like, but He had not yet come among us to really teach us how to play our individual instruments, or to conduct the orchestra. The score is a great gift, to be sure. It is, indeed, a masterpiece! But we still needed a teacher and a conductor to bring the music to life in our midst.

Incarnation

Then God fulfilled His promise. He came among us in human form, yet without diminishing His divinity. This occurred in the God/Man, the person of Jesus Christ, the Messiah of God. In the Old Testament God sent us a letter. In the New Testament He paid us a personal visit, so to speak. In the Old Testament He sent us an incredible score of His music. In the New Testament He personally taught us how to play it and conducts the orchestra Himself.

This Incarnation complemented and fulfilled everything in the Old Testament. The score is fulfilled and brought to life. The Conductor even makes some on-the-spot changes, which is His right, for He is also the composer. The Old is complemented and fulfilled in the New. The music jumps from the written page to the fingers and mouths of the musicians, and from there, to the spiritual ears and hearts of the listeners. God's beautiful music is actually heard in full form for the first time.

But the Incarnation not only complements and fulfills the formal Revelation of the Old Testament. It also complements and fulfills every major religion of the world. It complements all that is holy and good in every faith. It completes all that was still lacking.

This complement and fulfillment is far more wonderful and profound than simply claiming that our religion is better than someone else's. Many religions do this. It usually is counterproductive. This is more than simply claiming that "my dog is bigger than your dog," or "my music is better than yours."

Paradox and Paschal Mystery

It is true that the Catholic Christian perspective of the dying and rising of Jesus Christ provides the way to salvation through His bearing our sins upon the Cross and becoming the assurance of new life through Resurrection. On the objective level this is true. But that is not the only meaning of the Paschal Mystery. It is also mystical and stands as a doorway for our own dying and rising to a whole new way of being.

The basis of the complement and fulfillment of Jesus Christ is found in the ultimate expression of paradox, the Paschal Mystery. Every religion provides some kind of moral, belief-based compass to help its followers navigate the often confusing waters of life. There is much common ground even at this level among the faiths of the world, though there are also some significant differences. But the greatest area of convergence in Christ is on the level of mystery and paradox. Every religion worth its weight in salt also has a mystical tradition that tries to take humanity to its original and ultimate union with the Transcendent Reality. This Oneness with the One is found through paradox.

Here we are no longer taught objective, or knowable truths about Reality and the created, or temporal order. Here we are ushered into the place of pure mystery that can only be known through pure spiritual intuition, or unknowing. Here, we find wealth in poverty, exaltation in lowliness, proclamation in silence, communion in solitude, and so on. But beyond these paradoxes, the real union is found in a jump beyond the dualities of our phenomenal world. It is completely beyond the use of words, images, emotions, or senses, though we use all of those things to try to explain it. It is pure union and being.

Every major faith has a mystical, or wisdom tradition. In this, Jesus complements the other faiths of the world. Jesus joins unquestionably in the tradition of the Jewish prophets, the Hindu Sannyasin, the Buddhist Bodhisattva, the Taoist and Confucian sage, in his lifestyle and message. In this He is certainly commendable, but He is not really unique, except by His saintliness. Yet, Jesus probably would have looked a whole lot more like a Jewish prophet, a Hindu Sannyasin, a Buddhist Buddha or Bodhisattva, or a Taoist/ Confucian sage, than He would have looked like a Western mega-church pastor, or tele-evangelist/preacher (though these also have their place in the Church).

But He also does something no one has done before or since. He actually IS the teaching of the Paradox, and the Way, the Truth, and the Life, to mystical union with God beyond all concepts or words. This is done radically in the Cross and Resurrection. He no longer just teaches the Way. He no longer just practices the Way. In the paschal mystery He IS the Way. He simply IS, as God is the I AM. To use the analogy of music, He does not just teach and conduct the orchestra that makes the music of God. He IS the music, as He IS God. This is beyond our full objective understanding. It can only be grasped by mystical intuition of the spirit in His Spirit. This had never been done before. It has never been done since.

A comparison between the Buddha and Jesus might be helpful regarding any other holy person, or founder of other religions. The Buddha said that he was not the moon, but only a finger pointing towards the moon. This is appropriate for any mere human to say, enlightened or not. It is also appropriate for any priest or prophet. It is true of Lao Tsu, Confucius, and even Moses. In Jesus' humanity he would join the Buddha in this statement of humility when He said that He could only do what the Father gives Him to do. Yet, in the aspect of BEING the Reality of the Paradox, Jesus is not only a finger pointing towards the moon, or even the moon, but is the Light Who illumines the moon. In Catholic symbolism, the moon is the Church as typified by Mary. In this, Jesus joins with and complements the other teachers of the paradox. In actually being the paradox, He fulfills them all. It is not a statement of superiority or meant to evoke competition. It is actually a statement of joining with and complementing in the fulfillment. We affirm all that is good in the others in Christ.

Discipleship

Jesus attracted disciples. Just as with the other great masters, gurus, roshis, prophets, and founders of the religions of the world, Jesus called people to Himself and asked them to be initiated into discipleship. This initiation was through renunciation. Jesus called His first disciples to renounce all possessions, positions, and relationships in order to follow Him. This is radical, but also typical of all the religious and mystical masters. As Evagrios, the Christian monk and theologian said, we must, "renounce all to gain everything." Why is this so prominent?

I believe it all comes back to being able to hear and make God's music again with one's whole life. We have all fallen into patterns of orientation and behavior that are disordered. We have become part of the discord, beginning with our very being, and reaching out to the world through our words and actions. It's not that the things we use are always wrong. Sometimes we just use the right thing wrongly. This results in suffering and death. It results in discord and the death of God's harmony and peace. All humanity and all creation ultimately are affected and pay the price.

Specifically, this means letting go of the senses and emotions of the body and the thoughts of the mind or soul, in order to break through to the spirit. It usually begins with the senses of the body through physical asceticism, and then reaches out to emotions and thoughts through meditation. Since the old patterns have such a strong hold on us in these areas, we must sometimes make very intentional breaks with the patterns of the past in order to be reborn into the new. This is why the masters all demand complete renunciation at the beginning of conversion. Sometimes it is only for a time. Sometimes it is for life. But this renunciation of all enables us to be re-oriented towards a healthy use of our thoughts, emotions, and senses, with the spirit being unquestionably first in the order of priority regarding anything in our life. This includes not only the major things of morality and faith, but also, and even especially, the little things of mundane reality in our lives. When these little things become opportunities for the miracles of rebirth, then the big things can be approached without the danger of the old ego and self trying to sneak back in.

This is what the heart of the teaching of the Cross and Resurrection is about in Catholic Christian mysticism. We may use different meditation and prayer techniques to get there, as described by both East and West. But it is THIS that is the heart of the matter. Meditation remains simply a way to still the inordinate activities of the body and soul in order to awaken the spirit and ready it for rebirth. One by one we still the senses and emotions of the body through the use of stable posture and slow, even, and deliberate breath. This calms our whole person. Then we calm and focus the mind. Eventually we almost naturally pass over into the realm of the spirit in what we call contemplation in the Christian West. This is all done through the meditative actualization of the Cross and Resurrection of Jesus Christ for the Catholic Christian.

Other popular forms of meditation and prayer are also good. Charismatic prayer and praise tend to lift the individual out of their old self so that a new person can be reborn. The use of scripture, the Rosary, or litanies and novenas are good at redirecting the mind and heart towards the positive things of God, through the life of Christ and the attributes of God. All of these are excellent ways to redirect the person towards a breakthrough to the spirit beyond mere asceticism and meditation to pure contemplation.

So discipleship demands renunciation so that the discordant and chaotic priorities of body, soul, and sleeping spirit in the human person may be reordered according to the wonderful harmony of God. Then our whole life becomes His Music. Then we become His Song!

Church

When Jesus walked the face of the earth and called others to follow Him, they had to respond personally. But as soon as they did, they found themselves with other people who had responded to the same call. They found themselves in community. They found themselves in "the gathering," or *"ecclesia."* They found themselves in "the Church." That is all the word, "Church" means. It means the "gathering" of believers in Jesus.

Since Jesus brought the fullness of God's Music to the earth, it only made sense that there would soon be an orchestra to learn to play and to make the music. That is really all the Church is—an instrument of God's Song that can soothe and heal the world. It calls, teaches, and assists others in learning the Music of God as well. It turns us all right side up again so that we can be fully human once more—spirit, soul, and body.

The problem is, of course, that we do not always like all the people who have also decided to follow Jesus! In our old person, we would never have chosen to "hang out" with all these other people, and especially THESE other people! This is precisely where the challenge of making God's music for the world is really tested. As Barry McGuire says in concerts with me, "I wasn't looking to be a Christian. I didn't want to be Christian. I didn't even like Christians! In fact, I'm still working on that!" The audience roars with the laughter of recognizing their own experience of challenge in his words.

We may claim to have been remade according to the music of God, but unless we can also hear and play that music in and with others, we will never be able to bring a full-blown production of His Song to others. Then the world will never be able to hear the fullness of His music. Yes, there may be a lot of soloists gathered around, or a lot of composers and conductors. But unless we can join together with others in the orchestra, the music just remains notes on the page of the Divine Score, or partial performances of the whole at best!

It is here that the authenticity of our own reordering according to His teaching is really tested. If we let the Lord turn us right side up again, from body and soul with a sleeping spirit, to spirit, soul, and body, then we find a common union with all people and all creation by the very fact of this reorientation of living. When the spirit is really first in our lives, then we intuitively see and are united with this essence in all creation, animate and inanimate. Even if the others do not see it, we do. From this position of awakening and rebirth we begin to unite with others in their own potential for this reality whether they actually see it or not! From this communion, we also call it forth in all creation and in all the peoples of the world.

This takes great faith and patience, but it can be done. We actually call forth the hidden Spirit of Jesus in others when we act as Jesus would with them. This helps to spread the Music of God through Christ. This sings the Divine Song.

The harmony of God is also manifested in the call to discipleship within the Church that complements and fulfills the other faith traditions as well. Most traditions teach that a disciple must follow a teacher, a roshi, or a guru. Jesus is the Teacher of the Christian. Disciples in all traditions are called to renounce their possessions in order to break free from the habitual misuse of the things of the world at the beginning of their discipleship. Jesus also calls His disciples to renounce everything to follow Him. Even as the spirit of the guru is passed into the disciple, or the Dharma is transmitted through the roshi to the student, so does the very Spirit of Jesus, who leads us to all truth, pass into the Christian who really follows Him. As there is an authentic transmission from a succession of certified teachers from the Buddha on down to the present time in Zen, so there is a succession of apostles that Catholic and Orthodox Christians place themselves under to insure the authenticity of the teaching they receive from their elders.

Word and Sacrament

The Church is the instrument of God's grace. She brings us Word and sacrament. As we have said, this means that the Church teaches us the basic objective things about the morality and faith of life. She does this through her teaching authority as authentic successors to the Apostles, and especially Peter, who were called personally by Christ. But she also teaches and transmits the mystery. If anything, it is to this that all the rest is constantly pointing. This mystery is transmitted in two ways.

Though the word is a legitimate place for the objective teachings regarding faith and morality, it is also the place to call us into the mystery of Christ. As Christians, we are not "people of the book," we are "people with a book." We are people of the Word, the Incarnate Word. Jesus was the "Word made flesh." This Word is proclaimed in the silence between the words as much as in the words. It is proclaimed through spiritual intuition at work in that which is proclaimed, the proclaimer, and the listener. So the very holiness of the one who proclaims the Word formally is important, as is the holiness of those who take the Word in and embody it in their whole life, actions, words, and silences. This is something mystical.

It is the same with the music on the score of the written notes. You can do a technically impeccable performance of the notes, and totally miss the intention and spirit of the composer. If this is true with earthly music, how much more is it true with the music of the spirit and soul, the Music of God? We must proclaim and hear the Spirit, as well as the technical Word of God.

This leads us almost naturally to the sacrament. Here, the Word is not proclaimed by the mouth, the lips, or the tongue, they receive it! Here the proclamation occurs in the receiving, as well as in the giving of this wonderful gift. Here, the simple BEING of God through Christ in the sacrament proclaims the Word.

Among other things, "sacrament," simply means, "mystery." In the liturgy we often call the sacraments the mysteries. This is true especially of the Eucharist. It is the full embodiment of the whole Catholic Christian faith in a simple Presence, through a simple BEING of reality. It includes physical form in the matter. It also requires the form of a proclamation of the Word through the valid minister of the Church. But it moves beyond physical reality and the limitations of concepts and words, to the realm of pure BEING and Mystery. It IS, even as God IS, and Jesus IS the Incarnate Word.

Notice that in the Old Testament the Jewish synagogue beautifully reserves the scrolls of the Torah, the Word, in a tabernacle. In the New Testament, Christians still enthrone the scriptures in a special place on the lectern. But the tabernacle is now for a whole new kind of Word. It is an Incarnate Word. It has taken on the form and is under the appearance of bread, just as it was once incarnate in the flesh of Jesus born of God the Father and the Virgin Mary.

This is a music that can only be heard in silence. It is a liturgical action that leads one to sacred stillness, and extends that peaceful stillness out into all of the mundane actions of daily life. Good liturgy is a rehearsal for life. Good liturgy changes life and changes it for the better. If we can see our liturgy, Word and sacrament, in a whole new way through the rebirth of real spiritual intuition through Christ, then our whole life will soon be transformed as well.

Liturgy

Word and sacrament are housed within the liturgy of the Church. The liturgy is a journey from the senses and emotions of the body to the cognitive awareness of the soul, or mind, and from the soul to the intuition of essence in the spirit.

The liturgy begins with an experience of the senses of the body. This is so obvious that it is often over-looked. We begin by coming together in one place—the church building. The building itself is filled with sacred art, such as statues, paintings, and stained-glass win-dows. These all minister to the senses of the body. Furthermore, though we are joined together in one place, each individual must sit in a space in a pew that can be occupied by no one else. This symbolizes our unity and diversity in Christ and His Church. These are all sensual experiences and use the body as the begin-ning place of a spiritual journey.

The liturgy also appeals to the emotions of the body, keeping in mind that modern science tells us that emo-tions are primarily a chemical response to the senses and the mind. The entrance music is designed to stir us towards thanks and praise. During Lent it is designed to lead us to heartfelt contrition and repentance. We move almost immediately into the Penitential Rite, during which we bring closure to these emotions of contrition and repentance through forgiveness from God through the authority of the Church. It is unusual to see tears during the Penitential Rite. I believe this is because it is rushed through in a way that almost prohibits a full entering into its real meaning. All of this uses the emotions of the body to draw us closer to God.

The liturgy also ministers to the soul, or to the cognitive awareness of the mind, or spiritual thought. This is done through the Liturgy of the Word. This includes a formal proclamation of the scriptures by clergy and laity. But the formal proclamation of the Word does not conclude with the reading of the scripture aloud. The homily is preached by the bishop, priest, deacon, or extraordinarily appointed layperson, and represents the entire magesterium, or teaching authority of the entire Catholic Church. It is more than an exercise of the personal spirituality or theological opinions of an individual person. It is more than mere entertainment through the motivational preaching of the self-help guru. It is the teaching of the Church. It contains an intuitive mystical element that includes us all, but is bigger than any one of us alone. In this the liturgy ministers to and uses the soul to usher the individual and the congregation into the mystical place of pure spirit.

Finally, the liturgy takes us to the place of spirit beyond senses, emotions, or even spiritual thought. It is the place of pure mystery. It is the place of sacrament. This builds on the senses and emotions of the body, and the cognitive awareness and spiritual thoughts of mind and soul, but goes beyond them all. It is pure Oneness with He who IS. In this Oneness we enter into pure union with God, and communion, or common union, with the entire congregation, the entire Church, the whole human family, and all creation. Once this breakthrough occurs, all of the actions and emotions of body and the thoughts of soul become opportunities for continual enlightenment and rebirth in Christ. As the entire liturgy now becomes an opportunity for enlightenment and rebirth, so does liturgy become a rehearsal for all of life. As the liturgy becomes an exercise of enlightenment, so too does all of life become an opportunity for enlightenment and rebirth in Christ.

This walk through the liturgy has special importance in light of the interfaith environment of Catholics in the pluralistic religious environment of the United States and the entire West. Today it is not uncommon to hear people speak admirably of the "Liturgy Practice" of Buddhism. We also have such a tradition within Catholic Christianity. As Buddhism is on the rise in the West, we do well to rediscover our own wonderful tradition of approaching liturgy as a continuing process of enlightenment and rebirth in Christ.

One of the most basic things that we can do to rediscover the deeper beauty of liturgy and sacrament in our own Catholic faith is to simply *pray* the liturgy. This is an interior matter that has huge external ramifications.

We can also begin to employ some external tools that help to move us in the right direction.

The first is to *slow down* in our liturgical responses. The old saying is all too true that Catholics recite too fast and sing too slow! If we would slow down, we might actually have time to think and pray about what we say and to take a good deep breath as we do so.

When I visit parishes in my ministry, I find it impossible to keep up with the Lord's Prayer, the Creed, or Glory to God and other responses. I usually give up halfway through and resign myself to saying every third or fourth phrase or word. I am not alone in this experience. This is tragic and if it were not for the presence of many who sincerely pray the liturgy, despite its poor celebrative quality, our liturgies would actually border on blasphemy. Yes, they are that bad! If they were a movie or a concert, nobody would come. If they were a party, nobody would show up! Yet, if Jesus can show up, so can I, and He always does! He is truly present in the people, word, and sacrament, especially the Eucharist at every Mass, even the bad ones! While this is the great strength of Catholic worship, it can also be our greatest cop out. As the U.S. Bishops have recently said, "Good liturgy builds faith. Bad liturgy destroys faith." We want to build faith in Christ through our gatherings, and reach out with His good news to all the people of the world. So we must learn to *really* enter into the deeper reality of our liturgy.

Liturgy is the reestablishment of God's original music. It reestablishes the original peace and order of God's harmony, proportion, and rhythm. It takes us through body, to soul, to spirit, so that the spirit may be reborn in Christ and permeate through soul and body to reach the entire world. Once this occurs, each action, gesture, and word of the liturgy becomes an awakening experience in Christ. Each becomes a miracle to be revered. Once liturgy is reborn in this spiritual Music of God, then all of life becomes a miracle enlightenment and rebirth in Christ as well.

Conclusion

You may be asking, "this is all nice, but what does this have to do with music ministry?" I can assure you, it has *everything* to do with music ministry. Unless we can at least begin to hear God's music intuitively through the Church and the world, and everyone in them, then we cannot make God's spiritual music in a way that will really minister to others. No, we do not all have to be spiritual masters or mystics. If we wait for that nobody would have the courage to minister anywhere! We do, though, need to have some sense of these things and a real desire to grow in them before we start making the music that is supposed to lead others in that direction.

So, before we can make music *for* liturgy, we must hear and become, the music *of* liturgy. We can only do this when we place our whole life in discipleship to the

Master through the valid means of the Church. We must allow Him to reorder our whole orientation of life, right down to the way we think we are made, body, soul, and sleeping spirit, back to awakened and reborn spirit, soul, and body. Then we must make the radical break with the old patterns of our life that threaten to pull us back so the new can be protected and strengthened. Then we join with other brothers and sisters who are trying to do the same thing in order to be strengthened and to test the authenticity of our progress. Part of that communal process of the Church is the frequent, if not daily, celebration of Word and sacrament through the Holy Eucharist. Then our whole life begins to change. This is the Music of God.

Chapter 2

Biblical Basics

NOW that we have looked at the broad strokes of the analogy of the Music of God in the last section, let's look at some specific teachings regarding the use of music in the life of God's people. As we shall see, most of these come from the Old Testament, but the New Testament also gives some challenging applications. Furthermore, we shall discover that we often fall very short of the Old Testament minimums in our own use of music. If anything, according to our own beliefs about Christ and the Church, we should be far ahead after two thousand years! So such a look at scripture can be humbling.

Worship

The First Book of Chronicles gives us a lot of information about the use of music in worship in the Old Testament. In chapter 25 we read, "David and the officers of the army also set apart for the service the sons of Asaph, and of Heman, and of Jeduthun, who should prophesy with lyres, harps, and cymbals . . . under the direction of Asaph, who prophesied under the direction of the king."

This shows that the musicians involved in liturgical worship in the Old Testament were under the authority of an overall leader of the community.

The actual role of musicians seems rather obvious, especially in light of the Psalms of David. However, the Second Book of Chronicles gives some further insight into the spiritual importance and authority of the ministry of music in the liturgy. II Chronicles, chapter 5 describes the Dedication of the Temple. Solomon says, "Now when the priests came out of the holy place...and all the levitical singers . . . their sons and kindred, arrayed in fine linen, with cymbals, harps, and lyres, stood east of the altar with one hundred twenty priests who were trumpeters."

When the trumpeters and singers were heard as a single voice praising and giving thanks to the Lord, and when they raised the sound of the trumpets, cymbals and other musical instruments to "give thanks to the Lord, for he is good, for his steadfast love endures forever," the building of the Lord's Temple was filled with a cloud. The priests could not continue to minister because of the cloud, since the Lord's glory filled the house of God.

"Then Solomon said: 'The Lord intends to dwell in the darkness.' "

This scripture is awesome in its scope and ramifications for liturgical worship. First, it shows that there was a great unity between the musicians and priests that gave great power to the music that was created. They were heard as "one voice." Second, it manifests the power of praise in music, drawing everyone out of his or her negativity into the positive message of God. Third, and perhaps most importantly, it shows that liturgy is not an absolute manifestation of the presence of God. It is only a tool of God for the people of God. It is only a road sign on the journey of the soul and the Church to God. So often liturgists and Church musicians make a god out of liturgy. But liturgy is not God. It is only a tool of God to help the people of God worship God.

This scripture is the ideal reference for the charismatic, and the mystic, in relation to the purpose of music in liturgical worship and liturgical worship in general. It was liturgical worship music that seemed to call down, or stir up (to use the language of St. Paul's Second Letter to Timothy 1: 6,7) the presence of God symbolized by the language of His Theophony in the cloud. If you recall, God appeared in the pillar of cloud to the people of the Exodus from Egypt. This language is used again in the New Testament in the Transfiguration of Jesus on Mount Tabor (Mt17). The anonymous author of the Western spiritual classic, *The Cloud of Unknowing*, also uses it to describe mystical union and contemplative prayer. So, the presence of the cloud means that music has the ability to stir up the Spirit of God in a powerful way.

Also notice that, "the priests could not continue to minister because of the cloud, since the Lord's glory filled the house of God." The audacity of God to interrupt the liturgy! Seriously, the liturgy is God's gift to lead us into His sacred presence. Why should we not let God interrupt our schedule a bit, and take some time to simply enjoy His presence in our midst? Actually, this is called for in the rubrics, especially after Communion or after each psalm in the Divine Office.

I am reminded of the stories of the first Franciscans where a priest, Brother John of Alverna, had to stop in the middle of the consecration of the bread and wine into the Body and Blood of Christ during Mass because the presence of God drew him into a spiritual rapture that lasted until the following day! Stories like this abound in Franciscan lore and legend. I hear that it is also true of Pope John Paul II, who sometimes loses himself in a divinely touched moment, and reportedly has to be brought out of his raptured prayer in order to lead the congregation again. God frequently interrupts divine services and sacred schedules, in order to draw individuals and congregations into a supernaturally direct experience of His very Being and Presence. Music and liturgy are only gifts of God. When God uses them to reveal Himself in a supernatural way that is evident to all, then we should pause and enjoy the moment!

This scripture also sounds like Charismatic worship during a Eucharistic Liturgy. The liturgy and the spontaneous movement of the Spirit are not automatically opposed, as some would assume. They can be harmoniously brought together, if those in authority and in the congregation are truly open to the working of the Spirit. It is also very similar to liturgies where contemplative silence is *really* given the time and space to operate. Often the things that we think are opposed are really complementary, like two hands coming together to join in prayer. They can either clash or fold in the gesture of prayer. May such things always be like folded hands in the Church for genuine prayer.

One other related New Testament scripture that might be helpful relates the words of Jesus regarding worship. In John 4:24 we read, "God is spirit, and those who worship him must worship in spirit and in truth." We have addressed the aspect of "spirit" in the last section. Concerning truth, I have heard scholars say that this means not only objective truth, as in doctrine, etc., but also *reality*, as in the ultimate and deepest reality behind all things. That reality is the simple *being* of God. It is God's Spirit and our spirit in His. It is our being in His *being*. This means breaking through to the ultimate reality, the deepest and most essential center of all that is, be it God, humanity, or creation. This is done on the level of a feeling that is intuition rather than mere emotion, and truth that is the Ultimate Reality of absolute Being rather than mere thoughts and ideas. It is breaking through to the very spirit and essence of All that Is.

This has profound effects on the music we make and the way we make it. It basically means that worship music must come from the very deepest place of the human being and spirit. Since art is sometimes defined as the pure and essential communication of the deepest being and spirit of the artist through the medium of music, this means that worship music is potentially the most artistic form of music. It is a naked revelation of the composer and the performer in a way that draws the listener into that nakedness themselves. For the Christian musician this is done through the essential nakedness of our human spirit in the full revelation of God's Spirit. Through the medium of music, all is brought to the Light of Ultimate Reality in a total honesty and nakedness absolutely essential to authentic art.

What this means to me is quite personal. As a sacred music composer and performer, or musical prayer leader, this means I must spiritually become naked to God at every concert, liturgy, or private time of compositional musical prayer. This means that when I am before an audience or congregation, I am totally vulnerable before God. I must be able to totally lose myself in the music so that only Jesus may be visible. With John the Baptist I must decrease and He must increase. It also means that as a composer, I must first lose my self through prayer before I try to write one note or word. The songs flow naturally from prayer and return to prayer. Consequently, all of the normal problems of writing or performing, such as writer's block or stage fright, tend to disappear into the person of Jesus.

Of course what often hinders this potential in formal liturgy is the need for congregational music to also be singable, which requires it to remain fairly conservative musically. Some have said that worship music must move in big round and square figures, or "blocky," so that the congregation can figure out where it is going before it gets there. I agree. But it still must come from this deep place or it is not really worship music. It is just a functional time killer.

But this stylistic characteristic does not apply to music for devotional or meditational use, either privately or at appropriate times during the liturgy. Nor does it mean that even the most congregational song cannot reach from way down deep inside the composer and song leader and evoke something so deep as to be beyond words from the congregation, whether they sing along or just prayerfully listen.

So even congregational music holds the great potential for a most high expression of musical art. Unfortunately, this is rarely entered into. It is important for the worship music composers and song leaders to go there themselves, and then lead our brothers and sisters into that place of charismatic and mystical union with God and communion through Christ. But you cannot usher people to a place where you have never been. Spiritually, it would end up like the blind leading the blind.

True worship music has a profound effect on the faith and morality of lifestyle and spirituality. There are some related New Testament scriptures that deserve mention here. In chapter 2:16-3:17 of St. Paul's Letter to the Colossians, he goes to some length to describe Practices Contrary to Faith, Mystical Death and Resurrection, and the Practice of Virtues. This is a very similar pattern to what he does in his Letter to the Ephesians 4:25-5:20. Both letters include a journey from vice to virtue through the death and resurrection of Jesus and a life of praise and thanksgiving.

Of special interest to music ministry is the use of music in stirring these things up. Ephesians 5:19-20 says, "Be filled with the Spirit, as you sing psalms and hymns and spiritual songs. Singing to the Lord with all your hearts, giving thanks to God the Father at all times and for everything in the name of our Lord Jesus Christ." Colossians 3 says similarly, ". . . With gratitude in your hearts sing psalms, hymns, and spiritual songs to God." This last quote, in particular, is very rich in significance to the diverse use of music in music ministry beyond strict liturgy, but for this section we will confine ourselves to the topic at hand.

Both of these scriptures emphasize the role of music in stirring the "heart," which the early Church tells us means, not just the emotions, but the very core or spirit of our being. We have discussed this at some length above. Likewise, these scriptures tell us the importance of becoming people of praise with an attitude of gratitude. This is of special significance to musicians, who tend to be moody, melancholy people anyway. We can easily get stuck in negativity regarding many things.

To be a "person of praise" means that by faith we can see the work of God in everything, even those things we may consider "bad." Scripture tells us that, "We know that all things work together for good for those who love God, who are called according to his purpose" (Rom 8:28). This means *nothing* is beyond the control of a God who is essentially loving and good. "God is love," says I John 4:8. But what about the "mystery of evil?" God is in control even over the evil in our world. "I form light and create darkness. I make weal ("good" in some translations) and create woe ("evil" in some translations): I, the Lord do all these things" (Is 45:7). This does not mean that we begin to call good evil, and evil good. "Ah, you who call call evil good, and good evil ("woe to you" in some translations)" (Is 5:20). This does not mean that we praise Him *despite* evil things, as most of us would think. This means that we can praise Him *in* all things, and even *for* all things. The God of love and mercy leaves nothing outside of His loving control. This is meant to give us peace, not to make us resent God or feel constrained.

This opens a very mysterious topic that is beyond the scope, or space, of this little book (Rom 9:6-24). Suffice it to say that musicians, who so frequently tend towards becoming controlled by negative emotions, are actually called to lead people beyond that orientation into positive thoughts of praise and thanks, even in the midst of the ups and downs of life. We do this through our music, which is to be a naked expression of our own spirit and soul, so we must also experience this breakthrough ourselves to some degree.

But this is not just a matter of the benefits of positive thinking. It is a matter of actually stirring up the power of the Spirit of God in our lives. Psalm 100 says, "Enter his gates with thanksgiving, and his courts with praise." St Paul says to Timothy to "stir up," or "re-kindle" the gift that was given to him with the laying on of hands (2 Tim 1: 6). Applied to our lives, this means the gift of the Spirit given in the various sacraments and initiations in the Church. So, we stir up, or fan into a flame, the gift of the Spirit through songs of praise. Psalm 100 is a processional hymn. Do we use the procession at Mass as an active way to really stir up the Spirit of God in our midst, or do we simply use it as a way to get the procession down the aisle of the church with an appropriate song? The opening song can do both, but we frequently limit it to the latter through our own lack of praise and thanksgiving in our spirit and soul as we sing and play the song.

From these scriptures we can ask ourselves some final questions corresponding to the points above.

1. Do we really die with Christ before we try to enter into any ministry of music in the Church?

2. Is our music ministry team a united community within the greater Christian community in which we

find ourselves or are we divided among ourselves and with the community and leaders we are supposed to serve?

3. Are we positive people of praise and thanksgiving, or are we grumblers and complainers? Scripture is clear that we are to be a "people of praise" who have an "attitude of gratitude" to counter the negativity and darkness of our world. How can we lead others to such a spiritual doorway if we ourselves have not yet gone through it ourselves?

4. Do we allow the Lord to interrupt our lives with the extraordinary outpourings of his Holy Spirit, or do we limit God with the very tools he has given us to set us free? Do we approach our music with this kind of spiritual freedom, or do we bind ourselves, and consequently our congregations, by music which is designed, sung, and played by people who are still in bondage?

These are challenging questions that demand an answer.

Right now the liturgies of typical parishes in America are like many freeze-dried foods. They are easy to carry on a journey, but you must add water before they can be properly eaten and bring nourishment to the human body. That water is the Spirit of God.

As musicians we must open ourselves to His Spirit in the liturgical music we make before our liturgies can become spiritually reborn and awakened. We are losing young and middle-aged people in droves to the

New Age movement, meditation-oriented religions like Buddhism, and the Evangelical mega-churches where worship is vibrant and spiritually alive. Unless we bring the life of the Holy Spirit, as well as the mystical tradition of Mystery and reverence back into our liturgies, we will slowly lose everyone. I do not believe that is God's will! Our music has a very important role in bringing renewal to liturgy. Are we willing to pray and do the work needed to get it there? I hope we are. Nothing is impossible with God!

Prophecy

Scripture would teach us that music ministers do not only engage in worship and liturgical music; they also are involved in the ministry of the prophet. Biblical prophets do not necessarily mean those who foretell the future. They are literally "messengers" of God. In this they have a similar ministry to the angels.

So a prophet is simply a human messenger of God. They may be from any state of life, clerical, lay, or consecrated (religious). They hold no special institutional position in the Church, though many scholars believe that the early Church gave them the special honor to preside at Eucharist, as long as they were in good standing with the local bishop and did not take financial advantage of the community.

Our biblical text for this relationship between the ministry of the prophet and the sacred music minister is found in I Samuel 10, where the prophet Samuel is anointing Saul as King of Israel. After the anointing Saul is told, "as you come to the town, you will meet a band of prophets coming down from the shrine with harp, tambourine, flute, and lyre playing in front of them; they will be in a prophetic frenzy. Then the spirit of the Lord will possess you, and you will be in a prophetic frenzy with them and be turned into a different person. Now when these signs meet you, do whatever you see fit to do, for God is with you."

This scripture brings out two important aspects of music as ministry in the spiritual life. It is prophetic, and it is evangelistic. It aids in stirring up the "prophetic state," and it changes Saul into "a different person." This is challenging indeed!

Why does it aid in stirring up the prophetic state? I believe it is because it reaches down past externals to the deepest spiritual core of the human being and opens them up to receive the Spirit of God. Those, "who sing, pray twice," as the saying of St. Augustine goes. Music stirs the Spirit of God in a way that even preaching, despite its pre-eminence among the apostles, cannot do.

Notice that the prophets live and function in a "band" or community. Traditionally, prophets of this era lived under the direction of an elder prophet like Samuel, who taught them about the ministry. So, it is not necessarily enough to simply declare oneself a "prophet" and set out on a self-directed music ministry.

Traditionally, a beginner submitted to the training of those more experienced in the call of the prophet. This is also seen as one of the foundations of consecrated or early monastic life in the Church. While the bishops succeed the apostles within apostolic ministry, the monks or other more intense consecrations in the Church succeed to the prophetic office, though the clergy may also bear the prophetic anointing as a group or as individuals.

This means that the music minister must submit to good spiritual direction and the teaching authority of the Church. They should also seek ongoing musical training for the exercising of their craft. This takes time, the determination of faith, and great patience. A great music minister is not made in a day! Functionally, this means being willing to do the little things before we do the great. In the secular world of music, musicians are willing to do the "roadie" work just to get close to music. Slowly one works their way from learning from the masters, to finally perform, and *maybe* someday, to actually lead. Our music ministers need the same kind of preparation, determination, and humility.

An analogy might be helpful. To build a fine house one must learn the craft and have the right tools. Otherwise, one just ends up building a very inspired shack! Today, we have many musical "shacks" being built by well-intentioned music ministers who have never taken the time, effort, and patience to learn the deeper spirituality and quality of craft for their ministry.

To enter into the "prophetic state" requires that an individual have an openness to the charismatic and mystical gifts of the Spirit. Again, this requires a real "letting go and letting God" that lets go of self, and is able to move past subtle fear and inhibitions. It requires a great trust in God and the Church. Specifically, it requires a great trust in the community, or the charismatic and/or institutional elder who is the spiritual father or mother of the community. The latter is especially true of the newer communities in the Church where relationships similar to early monasticism are unfolding in our own day and time.

Many times we say to God, "Lord I will do anything for you "except this, that, or the other." As soon as "except" becomes acceptable in our language with God, we limit the full working of the Spirit in our life. The only "except" we should have is sin. This takes letting go of the old self through the dying and the rising of Christ.

The role of the prophet is not an easy one in the Church. It is not a road to glory but to being misunderstood and persecuted. Most of the prophets of both the Old Testament and New were not fully accepted by their own people. It is a delicate balancing act to remain truly Christian. Like Christ we are sometimes called to challenge our people and even the authorities of the Church. But we are never to do this in a way that challenges their God-given authority as successors to the apostles. We are always to remain humble before their office as pope and bishop. Nor are we to pull away from our brothers and sisters in the Church. This means that we may speak out through our music on a given topic. But then we must be willing to joyfully live with the consequences of our actions in the Church rather than to be separated from the Church. Nor can we do so grudgingly or with a secret judgment of others. We must give the word and then let go of ourselves in a way that truly brings the love, joy, and peace of one who has crucified themselves with Christ and opened the way for the full anointing of God's Spirit, and the rebirth of our spirit in Him. This is not easy. It takes great faith. It takes the faith of a prophet.

Evangelization

The other aspect of ministry brought out by 1 Samuel 10 is evangelization. Saul was "turned into a different person." This is the essence of evangelization: to shine the good news of Jesus Christ into other's lives in such a way for them to become more like Jesus in their own life. From an Old Testament perspective, this is what happened with Saul. It is also what happens to us when we really give our life to Christ.

Evangelistic music faces some unique challenges stylistically and spiritually. It must reach out to the culture of the world in which it finds itself without simply becoming "worldly." Usually this means the use of popular styles that might not be conducive to the more traditional music for worship. This can be seen in the recent phenomenon of Christian contemporary music. We also see this with many of the youth-oriented artists in the Catholic Association of Musicians. Specifically, the Life Teen program has used this approach to music in a most successful way, with some 500 parishes in the United States at the time of this writing. The Charismatic Renewal has also used more contemporary styles in its worship music. All of these are examples of using a more contemporary music to reach a more contemporary culture without losing themselves to a spirituality of worldliness.

The most successful of these examples is contemporary Christian music, which was actually birthed after consulting with Catholic musicians involved in the Folk Mass movement of the 1960s. It's true! The Baptists asked the Catholics how they put together contemporary folk music with traditional church worship in the "service music" of the Mass. They took it and ran with it, taking it inside and beyond the church doors, creating one of the most successful uses of music in evangelism in recent history. Catholics stayed primarily with liturgical use. What resulted was that we were stuck in the sixties, while our non-Catholic brothers and sisters in Christ took the gospel to the streets and to a whole new generation of believers. They drew them back into their churches with worship music they actually enjoyed! They also implemented programs of discipleship that, from their theological and ecclesial persuasion, were most successful. It is now time for Catholics to reclaim this music that we helped to birth! But there are challenges.

Catholic Christianity has some essential beliefs about the Church, the sacraments, and liturgy that are quite distinct, such as Jesus in the Eucharist, the structure of the Church through apostolic succession and the Pope, the communion of saints, and Mary's prominent role, just to name a few. These must be respected. Because of those beliefs, Catholics did not jump headlong into CCM (contemporary Christian music). Consequently, we did not make some of the mistakes of worldliness in the lifestyles and musical forms that our non-Catholic brothers and sisters made. We have a unique opportunity to do it a little better this time around. Nonetheless, if history is any indicator, we will probably make our own fair share of mistakes! But remember, in a good Catholic theology of "development of doctrine," these will also prove to be opportunities for further growth as well. They need not be feared.

Essentially, the use of contemporary musical forms is governed by the principle that forms are neither good nor bad. They are like natural laws of gravity. It is how we use them that make them good or evil. If the composer and the musicians are in union with God through the Spirit and prayer as they create the music, then the forms will generally be used properly. If not, they will become instruments of worldly attitudes and spirits, both for those who make the music and for those who participate.

But there are some forms that require the musician to get into a "place" that is at odds with the real gospel of Jesus. Frankly, I hear some of that in CCM today. I hope it does not creep into Catholic Contemporary Music as well. For example: I started out as a serious bluegrass banjo player. I was considered one of the up and coming players at the time. But to play the riffs that were cutting edge, I had to get into a place of mathematical precision that did not make me more like Christ. It made me machine-like inside. So, I let it go for the sake of another kind of music. Likewise, I was part of the beginnings of the country rock movement. I was playing acoustic, steel stringed guitar in a way that would later become quite popular before the "greats" had taken up that kind of playing. People still like to hear me play that way, and it is fun to do so. But God told me that this was not good as the main style for my music. This was for me personally. It placed too much attention on my playing and not enough on God. So I gave it up. Ironically, when we give up even the things that we are very good at in a worldly sense, God puts it together in a whole new way, and gives it back to us a hundredfold. In the end, my Catholic Christian music is far more successful than anything I did in secular music.

This also has spiritual significance regarding style and artistry. We may use contemporary style to reach a contemporary culture, but this sometimes borders on manipulation of style that results in bad art. Real art must flow from the inner depths of the artist. Otherwise it is just bad art. Likewise, if we go to the very deepest place in our being and make music from there, we will end up evangelizing even better than if we manipulated art in order to bring the things of the Spirit to a given generation or culture. This is more artistically and spiritually honest. It has integrity.

Back to our scriptural example from the story of Saul. It was the deeper worship music of the band of prophets that stirred up the Spirit that changed him into "a different man." They did not use secular techniques in order to reach him. No. They went right to the deepest core of spirituality in music as a catalyst to change Saul into the man he needed to be for God. With me, I have found that I reach far more people for Christ, the Church, and vocational calls in the Church, when I simply go to the deepest place of the Spirit in my musical composition and performance and let God take care of the rest.

I am reminded of he time I asked Barry McGuire, one of the early fathers of CCM, how to make Christian music. I had used all of the techniques I learned in secular music when I began my music ministry, and they were not working well. Barry gave me some advice that would change my music ministry forever. He said, "When you make Christian music, play to God not to the people. God will take care of the people, for He can do it better than you can!" Those words changed my music and helped to change my life for the better in Christ.

Teaching

We have already shown why music is so helpful in assisting the various ministries of the Church. It stirs up the deepest places of soul and spirit so that the Word of God may find a receptive place within. But it can also be used as a direct tool for teaching.

St. Paul's letter to the Colossians implies the use of music in the teaching ministry of the Church. In Colossians 3:16 Paul says, "Let the word of Christ dwell in you richly. Teach and admonish each other in all wisdom; and with gratitude in your hearts sing psalms, hymns and spiritual songs to God." So music is connected to the ministry of the catechist.

This has stylistic applications. Again, we simply use the contemporary to reach our contemporaries. But some styles are more appropriate for teaching. Folk music, for instance, has been used as a vehicle for the pop poets of our time, like Bob Dylan or Jackson Browne. Today, even some rock styles are more "folk" in their function and feel than they are pure rock. Another style that is not easily accepted by many traditionalist Christians is Rap. Rap has an enormous capacity for the lyric that is not found in other styles. We may or may not personally enjoy Catholic Rap, but I have heard more actual teaching of Catholic doctrine and dogma in Rap than I have in any other contemporary form.

Now, as a more mystically oriented artist and the Founder of the Catholic Association of Musicians (CAM), I must also state my own cautions and fears about too quickly accepting all of these contemporary forms into mainstream Catholic music, which could inadvertently let a Trojan Horse into the Church. That horse is the horse of worldliness. I have seen CCM make terrible mistakes in this regard. What started out as a genuine desire to reach a contemporary generation with the gospel through music produced an entire generation of Christian music that is now more worldly than Christian. You can see it in the music, the business ethics of the industry it produced, and in the lifestyle of the artists themselves. Of course, these are generalizations and happily suffer from the many exceptions to the rule in truly fine music and people in CCM. Nonetheless, I am afraid that instead of reclaiming a successful music ministry approach, we may simply imitate the mistakes of our non-Catholic brothers and sisters in Christ. CAM has attempted to address most of these issues through its statutes.

Healing

Not long after Saul was anointed as King of Israel, he began to fall out of the favor of the Lord by his disobedience to the instructions of God from the prophet Samuel. Specifically, this was about Saul performing the ritual sacrifice before battle instead of waiting for Samuel, who was designated to perform the sacrifice. Interestingly, Samuel was very late, and Saul thought he was fulfilling rather than breaking the law. Furthermore, Samuel was a prophet not a priest, although raised by a priest in the temple. Saul went on to use the spoils from the battle to build up his treasury instead of destroying everything as God had commanded. Suffice it to say that Saul had clearly disobeyed the word of God for him. Consequently, God reproved him through the prophet Samuel saying, "I regret that I made Saul king, for he has turned his back from following me, and has not carried out my commands." To Saul he said through Samuel, "Because you have rejected the word of the Lord, he has also rejected you from being king" (I Sam.15:11,23). Samuel secretly anoints David the new King at God's command, though Saul continues to act as King. But Saul knew God had rejected him as King. Needless to say, Saul was not feeling very good by this time! A spirit of melancholy overtook him.

In 1 Samuel 16:14-23 we read, "Now the spirit of the Lord departed from Saul, and an evil spirit from the

Lord tormented him." One of his assistants said, "Command your servants to look for someone who is skillful in playing the lyre, and when the evil spirit from God is upon you, he will play it, and you will feel better." Of all people, they find the shepherd boy that Samuel had anointed, David, and bring him to minister to the popularly recognized King. The text continues, "And whenever the evil spirit from God came upon Saul, David took the lyre and played it with his hand, and Saul would be relieved and feel better."

This scripture brings out another aspect of music ministry: healing and deliverance from evil spirits. Ironically, we do not get any indication that these were songs with words. It only mentions playing the harp, though I suppose, in light of the many psalms of David in scripture, words might also have been involved.

I know that my music is frequently used in healing ministry. Sometimes this simply amounts to playing my recorded music during prayer or daily activities. Sometimes it involves my live music. I recall a woman who once traveled to all my concerts around the country. At first it scared my team. They thought she was stalking me. Then we talked to her and found out that she came to my concerts because it was cheaper than professional therapy, and seemed to work better for her.

But professional therapists of all sorts also use my recorded music during sessions. These range all the way from Christian psychiatrists and psychologists, to massage therapists and chiropractors, to medical doctors of all sorts. The music apparently helps to get people into a relaxed place so that God can work to heal their bodies, emotions, and thoughts. I am an honorary member of The Association of Christian Therapists, even though I don't have a degree as a therapist in any of those particular healing arts. I am always a little amazed at how God works!

This music can also be used during liturgy. There are specific times where meditational music is appropriate and even called for. One such place is after Communion. However, some caution has to be used here as well. After receiving the greatest ongoing sacramental gift for the Catholic Christian in the most intimate way and place in our soul, our music must *never* intrude upon the sacredness of those precious few moments of silence and stillness during a Mass. Throughout the rest of the liturgy the individual is called out of themselves to participate with others in the congregation. This is a sacred time of intimacy between each individual and Jesus. Any music used here must be gentle and unobtrusive; it must draw the listener into greater communion with Jesus and the Church in an intimately interior way. Only then can that intimate experience be shared with others as we move out of the Church and into the world as Mass concludes, and we are sent forth as heralds of the good news.

Conclusion

So we can see that scripture calls the music ministry of the Church to a diversity of applications. Worship, liturgy, prophesy, and healing are already implied in the Old Testament. Teaching is added in the New. This all has a profound effect on the spirituality of the musician and the style of music they use. Up until now, the Catholic Church of this era has yet to really explore and formally support these applications. We have kept our music isolated to a rather functional mode during liturgy. I believe this is at least one reason that our liturgies are often so uninspiring to those seeking deeper spirituality.

But the Church cannot support what it cannot see or hear, and it cannot see or hear such music ministry if it is not being brought forth. It is up to the musicians themselves to open themselves to God's creative power and bring forth just such music and ministry. It is now time for the musicians to rise to this vocational challenge. The challenge is to a greater spirituality and professional quality than we have ever known in our generation. Awake, O sleeper! It is now the hour to wake from your sleep!

The New Testament ends with several mentions of music that seem an appropriate way to end this section. They are found in the Apocalypse, the Revelation to John, and speak about the final music in heaven.

"The twenty-four elders fell before the Lamb, each holding a harp and golden bowls full of incense, which are the prayers of the saints. They sing a new song: 'You are worthy to take the scroll and to open its seals' . . . I heard the voice of many angels surrounding the throne and the living creatures and the elders; they numbered myriads of myriads and thousands of thousands, singing with full voice, 'Worthy is the lamb that was slaughtered' . . . Then I heard every creature in heaven and on earth and under the earth and in the sea, and all that is in them, singing, 'To the one seated on the throne and to the Lamb be blessing and honor and glory and might forever and ever!'" (Rev 5:8, 11-13).

Such scenes are repeated frequently throughout the Apocalypse, the unveiling and Revelation of heavenly *reality*. All through this book God's people in heaven are singing. But they do not sing alone. They sing with the angels in communion with those of us still left on earth in spiritual battle. It is the Communion of the Saints and angels. What does this mean?

I believe it means Eternal Music like we spoke of at the beginning of this book. As the wall in heaven is, "pure gold, crystal clear," and as the streets are, "pure gold, like transparent glass," so is this music something we can hear, but it is beyond normal hearing. As some mystics have said, "There you can see sound and hear color." It is a matter of simply *being* the Music of God. This Eternal Music is sung by all creation by simply being. We will spend all eternity making this Music of God's harmony, proportion, and rhythm by simply being with He who IS. The great breadth, and width, and depth of our call in the Church today is only a glimpse of what lies ahead. It is just a rehearsal for the *Real Song*. If we begin to get to that place in our music now, we will be well rehearsed by the time we get there!

Chapter 3

Church Teaching

CATHOLICS believe that we are given the teaching of Jesus Christ through the threefold ministry of Scripture, Tradition, and Magesterium. Apostolic Tradition is the written and oral strain of the teachings of the apostles as passed down through their successors to the ages. Scripture is the earliest authoritative written account of Apostolic Tradition, and forms the "Canon," or, "yardstick," by which any further development of Apostolic Tradition is measured. Magesterium is the formal teaching authority of the Church through the successors to the twelve apostles under the guidance of Simon Peter in the persons of the bishops and the pope. A true knowledge and awareness of the documents of the Church regarding sacred music is most helpful for anyone engaging in music ministry within the Church.

By and large through the last century the Church has developed from a more exclusive use of music in the liturgy, to something more inclusive. The exclusive use limited sacred music to Gregorian chant, polyphony, and a most careful use of classical modern music, but was quite articulate and refined in its theology of sacred music. Slowly, the Church began to accept modern and even secular forms, especially in mission circumstances, as long as proper reverence and respect for sacred liturgy was retained.

The main sources are as follows:

Pope Pius X, *The Restoration of Church Music (Inter Sollicitudines)*, 1903

Pope Pius XII, *Encyclical on Sacred Music in the Liturgy (Musica Sacrae)*, 1955

Vatican II, *Constitution on the Sacred Liturgy (Sacrosanctum Concilium)*, 1963

Pope Paul VI, *Instruction on Sacred Music (Musicam Sacream)*, 1967

Music in Catholic Worship, 1972, Revised, 1982

Liturgical Music Today, 1982

Bishops Committe on the Liturgy

United States Catholic Conference

These documents provide a wealth of direction that is consistent and clear regarding the general use of sacred music for the Church. It also shows a particular development that is universally solid but open to adaptation in particular applications of the general norms. It gives the current Church documents on sacred music an historical context from which to be read.

The following summary will hopefully be helpful regarding the topics raised in this book. I will also

add some comments from my experience in music
ministry.

Music as Sacred Art

The first thing we notice is that "sacred music" is
both "art" and "sacred." The documents are clear that
sacred music is art in the fullest sense and of all
sacred art, music is considered the most sacred. This
is largely due to its great compatibility with use during sacred liturgy. A principle that the more music is
associated with the liturgy the more sacred it becomes, is most evident in the earlier documents. But
it is still true today that the liturgy is the highest
expression of the assembled people of God, and
therefore sacred music used for liturgy is the highest
of music ministries.

Training

The sacred music composer and artist are, therefore, to be highly trained and fully competent on both
the artistic and spiritual levels. They are properly
trained in the science and art of music, and specifically in the history and spirituality of sacred music. They
are also sufficiently trained in the more overt sacred
studies of doctrine, theology, and liturgy. Lastly, their
lives correspond to their studies and their songs in an
appropriate level of holiness in Christ. A musician must
understand and live the "sacred" in Christ and the

Church, before they can be a "sacred" music minister in the Church.

The sacred music minister is, indeed, to be a "minister." Training and holiness of life are required to engage in this ministry. Interestingly, in the earlier documents of the 20th century, Church musicians were to be appropriately vested during liturgy to emphasize that their role was sacred and ministerial. This is still seen with the use of choir robes today. While the priest/celebrant is the normal presider over the liturgy, the sacred music minister is a valid, but non-ordained, minister of the Church.

Authority

But just because one is a "minister" of the Church does not give one the right to be autonomous from legitimate Church authority on the international, national, or local levels. The music ministry, and those within it, exists under the greater authority of the pastor of the parish and the liturgy committee they oversee. Likewise, every diocese has a Liturgical Commission to assist each parish and community in celebrating liturgical worship with the highest quality possible in the service of God and God's people.

The sacred character of music is proportional to its involvement with the liturgy, especially the eucharistic liturgy. Because of their extended and highly successful use throughout the history of the Church, Gregorian and Byzantine chant are seen as the most sacred in character among all other forms of music. Polyphony is also seen as part of this primary tradition. So the original chants of the Church are to be respectfully and lovingly maintained and nurtured in today's liturgies. But practically speaking, this is in stark contrast to the actual practice of most parishes in America. As a musician and a convert to the Catholic faith, I personally believe this is a great and tragic loss.

Gregorian Chant

It is true that Gregorian chant holds a pre-eminent place, not only in sacred music, but also in music in general. Its graceful lyric and tones have an uncanny ability to transport the listener to a truly spiritual place, whether they are believers or not! This ability has been recognized by many as being unrivaled by almost any other musical style in western, or even global history. Furthermore, in our tradition there are studies into the use of the different modes for each of the liturgical seasons that bring out the effect of various musical tones and modes upon emotion, mind, and spirit. Such studies have yet to be completed from a Christian perspective with modern music, though there have been great advancements in this field by those engaged in Ambient music and Asian orchestral music, and its use for emotional and physical healing.

But official documents also show that Gregorian chant was once the "new music" of the Church of the Roman Empire. Furthermore, it was a bold step to include the vernacular, or the language of the people, in a liturgy that had primarily been in Greek and Middle Eastern languages until around 800. Contrary to popular belief that Gregorian chant materialized from heaven in one divine form, the documents of the Church confirm that it evolved very slowly, taking almost one thousand years to come to us in its present form. No doubt, there were a lot of chants left on the scriptorium floors, or in the back shelves of the libraries of monasteries and cathedrals across Christendom! Ironically, instead of Gregorian chant being a symbol of inflexibility, its inclusion in the Catholic Church is actually a sign of adaptation and change to reflect Christianity within the various cultures of the world.

Because of this the Church has, in an appropriately discerning way, been open to new forms of music in the liturgy. First, she began to accept polyphony, or music with an interwoven fabric of autonomous melodies forming primitive harmonies and chords, rather than the single melodies of Gregorian chant. Because it was sung unaccompanied, this music still retains much of the character of chant. Then she began to accept hymns and other sacred songs based on the more modern musical developments of the classical period.

Instruments

Another development was the use of the pipe organ, and later the electronic organ, during liturgy. The organ has always been seen as most compatible with chant and hymns, due to its ability to go from very soft to very loud dynamics in a non-abrasive way. The Church also began to accept bowed instruments such as the violin and hand bells as appropriate. What is important here is an understanding of having the proper attitude of worship, praise, and prayer when playing any instrument in the church. The documents also specify that instrumental music is acceptable at certain points of the liturgy, such as the Presentation of the Gifts.

Profane Elements

During the Middle Ages there was a careful attempt to keep anything "profane" from sacred music. Consequently, any instruments or styles associated more overtly or exclusively with secular music and entertainment were cautiously avoided. While this may seem unusual from our perspective in time and culture, it was a common phenomenon throughout all of Christianity. What is relevant to us today is the awareness that certain attitudes of composition and performance are irreconcilable with the fruits of the Spirit: love, joy, patience, kindness, generosity, goodness, mildness, chastity, and faith. This awareness makes certain styles very difficult for sacred music musicians to play.

Non-Liturgical Religious Music

Later, the Church began to accept "religious music," or music with a religious lyric and theme, but with a melody and mode more commonly associated with popular, or secular music. The Church highly applauded this religious use of music to reach the people of a particular culture, but she still kept this music from being used during liturgical worship. Such religious music was encouraged for use in theaters, performance and concert halls, or in other more secular places. This is highly significant regarding the phenomenon of Contemporary Catholic Music and its use in evangelization outside of the church building today.

Though not a formal Church teaching, I am reminded of the use of Mystery Plays by the Franciscans in medieval Europe. They would make use of popular religious music, dance, and drama in the streets and lawns just outside of the cathedrals and churches of Europe to attract large crowds through religious entertainment. Then they would lead them into the cathedrals and large churches to celebrate the Eucharist. This was a marvelous combination of the sacred and the secular in a true religious spirit that can renew all of society through Christ.

Missionary Music

From the beginning the Church always recognized the missionary need to use the music of a particular culture in order to reach the people of that culture. She also recognized the general religious character of the music of the various religions in cultures to which the missionaries went. Consequently, missionaries were encouraged to use the popular, or even adapted indigenous religious music of the people in order to reach them,even during liturgy. Only later, as the people assimilated Christianity comfortably, were they encouraged to learn the more ancient chants and Church hymns.

Of course, by today's standards this would be viewed as culturally colonial in attitude and would not be so readily endorsed. Still, this has a huge significance for us regarding the use of contemporary music in Catholic worship today in order to reach our substantially non-Christian contemporary culture. We have become missionaries in our own post-Christian culture.

Contemporary Music

More recently the Church has opened its doors to contemporary music, as long as it is truly compatible with the reverent spirit and harmonious function of the liturgy. Hymns, responsorial singing, folk, gospel, and other contemporary styles are considered compatible as long as the appropriate conditions judged fitting by the local bishop and his counsel are met. The rise of renewal movements like Cursillo and the Charismatic Renewal, just to name two, have helped popularize and bring acceptance of these more contemporary musical expressions of worship, praise, and prayer. Significantly, in a true ecumenical gesture of humility, Catholic musicians and composers are to research and learn from, not only overt Catholic music, but also the musical traditions of other Christians as well. The above-mentioned movements have helped in this regard, as well as others.

Specifically, the Church has recently recognized the usefulness of contemporary music in reaching the youth. This has been especially emphasized during the World Youth Days celebrations during the Pontificate of Pope John Paul II. Furthermore, the need for contemporary music during youth masses and for gatherings of youth movements, has been readily endorsed by the Church, as long as this does not create a spirit of division within a given parish or diocese. This is very clear in the documents. Organizations like Life Teen have proven that this can be done most effectively, though, as with any movement in the history of the Church, they occasionally face issues that must be worked through by the grace of God and the help of the Church.

Specialized Call

While the Church recognizes that the primary body of singing worshippers during the liturgy is the congregation, or assembly, she also recognizes the unique ministry of the cantor and choir. Consequently, she encourages only those with musical talent, basic musical and spiritual training, and appropriate holiness of life to be received as formal sacred music ministers. Simply put, if you cannot play or sing well you probably should not be in the music group! Furthermore, just because you can does not mean that you should! Spiritual and emotional maturity are needed before we are ready to engage in any ministry in the Church. We best submit this judgment to those in authority, rather than trying to make them on our own.

Choir

Ideally, every parish should have a choir. This is a group of qualified singers of sacred music. Most good parishes have a traditional choir, a children's choir, and a contemporary choir. Of course, a choir usually needs a choral director, or a leader. Likewise, there should be an organist for traditional services and other instrumentalists for the more contemporary liturgies. In a large church some of these are full-time positions, especially that of the overall music director. When this is missing the liturgies can suffer, and as the documents say, "good liturgy builds faith, bad liturgy destroys faith." Parishes no longer have the luxury of skimping on the music budget. It is of utmost importance.

Cantor

There should also be a cantor. This is the soloist who leads certain parts of the liturgy, such as the Responsorial Psalm after the first reading during the Liturgy of the Word. The Church would also recognize the use of solos in other places, such as during the Preparation of the Gifts, or as a Communion meditation. In the case where there is no choir the Cantor may lead all of the music. But this should be seen as extraordinary, due to circumstance, and not normative.

Physical Placement

The physical placement of the cantor and choir has also been an issue for much discussion in recent years. In times past the choir was usually placed in a choir loft in the back of the church next to the organ. Musically this was quite helpful, due to the close proximity of the choir and the organ. It also worked with the more "otherworldly" style of liturgical worship and music. But recently, with the advent of liturgical changes that saw the choir as part of the congregation and with the development of more contemporary styles and configurations that work best with some eye contact with the people, they are frequently put up front and to one side of the sanctuary and main altar area. In the newest churches the choir is placed outside of the sanctuary, so as to emphasize the participation of the congregation with the choir, but still visibly prominent enough so as to facilitate leading the congregation in song. This works well, except when the choir is actually placed too far to the side of the congregation, thus impeding the visibility or eye contact. This is a case where it is liturgically correct, but functionally missing the point. Of course, physical restrictions dictate flexibility in implementing this.

Electronic Media

The Church has also considered things as functionally mundane as the use of P. A. systems, lighting, the use of recorded music, and television and radio in the parish. When these documents were written such topics seemed "cutting-edge," but now they are commonplace. Simply put, the Church encourages a good, but nonintrusive, use of technical and media equipment. When liturgy becomes a media performance instead of a true service of prayer, something has gone terribly wrong! Recorded music may be used, but the singing and playing of real people is always preferable in the worship of a real God! But even here, the use of sampled and synthesized sound creates new ethical and moral issues. Personally, I always prefer live acoustic sound to sample or synthesized patches. But I also realize that financial limitations are sometimes an issue. Therefore, the limited use of synthesized or sampled sounds to replace live acoustic performance is sometimes unavoidable. Furthermore, some synthesized sounds are unique, and therefore have integrity in themselves. In that case their use is completely justifiable.

Financial Compensation

Finally, and perhaps most uncomfortably, is the issue of financial compensation. The documents are clear that those who work for the Church should be fairly compensated. True, some of this compensation is spiritual. No other employer can offer this compensation quite so effectively as does the Church. But we also live in a material world, and our musicians and composers have to pay bills like the rest of us. Therefore, it is only fair and right to offer financial compensation for their work. Usually, a church needs at least one full-time music minister on staff, if not more. Some musicians are best paid part time, or by the performance. The use of the musicians' union is usually not necessary for church work, but it should be investigated in the region in which the church is established. Furthermore, the documents are also clear about paying appropriate royalties and copyrights for use of printed sheet music and recorded songs. There are now plenty of good companies dedicated to helping the music ministry of parishes so that this need no longer be an issue. As a composer, I can confirm that it is most discouraging when well-to-do parishes use copyrighted materials in an illegal fashion. Usually this is done out of ignorance, but with today's teaching from the Church, there is really no longer any excuse. We cannot expect the many fine composers and artists who struggle financially, to continue to perfect their craft for our spiritual benefit if they are not at least fairly compensated for their work.

Spirit and Law

Ironically, some of these rather strong documents end with an equally strong reminder that, while these liturgical policies and laws are important, they are not as important as the spirit behind the legislation. This is an awareness of the old theological balance between law and Spirit. The law without the Spirit is oppressive, while the Spirit without the law can lose direction. When both work together there is balance and harmony in all things. This is always the highest goal of the Church in addressing such things. The harmony and balance of Jesus is to be evident in the liturgy of the Church itself and in the lives of her members.

So the Church has given us some serious teaching regarding the many and varied aspects of sacred music ministry. We have only looked to the last century, and I have only mentioned some areas of the teaching. The documents also give clear and concise teaching about the more general aspects of liturgy. At various periods of time in the last century they have also gone through every part of the liturgy and addressed the musical issues of each in a way consistent with the theology and practice of the Church at the time. However, it isn't easy to discern a general vision and direction in the overall body of the documents. The later documents are especially helpful to those of us engaged in sacred music ministry in the typical Catholic parish today. I encourage you to refer to them for confirmation and broadening of your current understanding and practice of this wonderful ministry of sacred music.

Chapter 4

The Master Musician

A FTER the preceding overview of sacred music through consideration of the general Music of God in the Church, humanity, and all things, the biblical basics, and some general Church guidelines, we now look more specifically to the actual styles and configurations of church music. We will do this by summarizing some of my analogies and teachings from my previously published book, *The Master Musician*. God is the Master Musician. We learn from Him how to play the instrument and sing the song. I believe they might be helpful here.

The Instrument

The Master Musician begins with consideration of the analogy of our initial spiritual life in Christ with the making of a guitar from a tree in the forest. The tree must be totally cut down before it can be used in the creation of a fine musical instrument. After it is cut down it must be cut into pieces, dried, shaped, assembled, and finally sanded and varnished many times. All of this is a simple analogy of the initial, and ongoing dying to our old self and rising to a whole new person to be a fitting instrument to make God's Music and Song.

I was trained to make popular folk and rock music, and I achieved national success in the newly forming country rock idiom of the late 1960s and early 1970s in a band with a cult following called Mason Proffit. When I went through an adult conversion and began to seriously follow Christ, I wanted to make sacred, or Christian music. At first I simply used the secular style I was trained in with the addition of Christian lyrics. This worked well at first, but proved ineffective with further spiritual progress.

After I became Roman Catholic and seriously pursued the monastic and Franciscan way of life, I found that I had to give up my entire old way of life to go deeper in Christ. This included my music. I moved into a hermitage in the woods at a Franciscan retreat center, and gave up everything, including my music. Only after I did that did God give me back a whole new way of life. I became the Founder of the Brothers and Sisters of Charity at Little Portion Hermitage. He also gave me a whole new music, with an entirely new style, that far surpassed the spiritual, artistic, and even the commercial accomplishments and success of my previous secular career. When we die to the old self through the cross of Christ, God does give us back a whole new way of life through the Resurrection of Jesus that far surpasses anything we could possibly expect or imagine!

The Musician

But the above analogy of crafting a fine guitar from a tree is not the end of the process. It is only the beginning! We are not only to be a fine musical instrument. We are to become master musicians as well! The further analogy of learning how to make music also applies to the various aspects of training in styles and configurations of modern sacred music.

I have often heard it said that the tone of a great musician is found, not so much in the quality of the instrument but in the fingers themselves. So, good tone is not only in the instrument. It is in the fingers! But in order for good tone to be found in the fingers, it first must be found in the heart. To be maintained in the heart it has to be practiced through years of listening and training found in every note of every song.

The great musician must truly love music. It is not enough to learn to play the notes in a way that is technically correct. One must learn to find the spirit behind the note. One must learn to hear Eternity in every note. For the singer of sacred song this is also true of every word. In this way music becomes sacramental. In this way we become musicians, not just musical technicians.

But the great musician must also do the hard work of learning the theory, musical scales, and exercises.

They must be played over and over. This takes time and hard work. But this is so they can become second nature, and can be played without conscious thought about each note. The musician simply says to himself "play," and he effortlessly plays the necessary scale. In this way he can concentrate on the spirit and the emotion behind notes, rather than on the notes themselves. This is symbolic of doing the work of asceticism and theology in our religious life. As scripture instructs, "embrace discipline, and when you are old she will support you like a throne" (Sir 6:18-37). As St. Benedict teaches, while this discipline may be difficult at first, after many years it becomes second nature and frees us up for deeper mystical things of God.

The great musician must also study the various musical, cultural, and spiritual traditions that have created the different theories and styles of sacred and secular music. This takes great humility and poverty of spirit. We must learn other traditions in order to discover that which is uniquely our own. This symbolizes the need to study the many spiritual traditions that precede us in order to truly be confident of our own place in the overall tradition of the Church today. This has been the genius of the saintly founders of religious congregations. It is to become ours as well.

All of this means that we must learn the balance between form, freedom, and power. For instance, in playing the guitar one begins by learning the proper posture in holding the instrument. The proper posture may seem artificial and uncomfortable at first. But months and years later, that same posture will enable us to play more difficult positions, scales, and musical pieces with greater comfort and ease. Learning the proper form at the beginning unleashes greater power at the end. This is like learning the classical forms of faith in doctrine, sacrament, ecclesiology, mystical prayer, and traditional monastic or consecrated life. It is like studying under a novice master to become a good monk of a monastery or community, or under a gifted catechist as a catechumen to become a full member of the Church.

But after all of the study and practice, one comes into one's own. We "find our voice." After studying the vocal styles of many others and copying them in our own performance, one day, out of nowhere, we find a voice that is uniquely "ours." For myself, I imitated the singing and playing of countless popular folk and rock composers and artists. Then one day, after letting go of all of it through Christ, I found my own style and sound. The same is true in our spirituality. After years of practice, we suddenly find our own "sound," or ministry and call. It complements all that came before, but it has become something unique and new.

We must also find the balance between words and music in writing our own song. As love and truth come together in Spirit to give us Jesus, so must scripture and prayer come together in the Spirit to give us a sacred song. This means we must become proficient in the working knowledge of scripture and in the practice of prayer. This is also true in the spiritual life. It is like the two wings of spiritual flight. When we find the right balance between study and prayer, we find the two wings that can cause us to soar to the heights of the mystical life. It is also like the oars of a spiritual boat. When the two oars are balanced you can go forward on a steady course until you reach your destination.

Similar to the analogy of practice, the memorization of lyrics, melodies, and chords frees us up to enter into the spirit of the song. It must become second nature. This is like the schedule and discipline of a particular community becoming second nature to the novice, so that they may someday become truly mature members who enter into the deeper spirit of the gospel in every community.

Styles

It is also important to identify the various musical styles of sacred and secular music and to study them with great love and devotion. This is called, "musicology." Such devoted study helps us to become more confident in our own style and to understand our own identity better. It helps our music to become an authentic instrument of love.

We must be careful, however, to avoid the treacherous trap of missing the beauty and joy of music in the practice of musicology, or the study of music. Many unintentionally limit the creativity of the musicians of our day by judging them against the mere technical standards of the music of those from another culture and time. Worse yet, many judge the musicians of our own day by the external technicalities of the music of the past, miss the spirit of the music or the musicians of today, and are actually unable to successfully make any creative music themselves. Though there are people called to the legitimate ministry of the critic, this can be a most dangerous trap for the critics themselves. In the Church this is like those who study the lives of the saints and judge those who are seeking to become saints today by technical and external standards alone. They totally miss the spirit of today's saints while failing to become saints themselves! This is a great hypocrisy and a terrible tragedy. As Jesus said of the hypocrites of his own day, some who build the tombs of the prophets would be the same ones to kill prophets in their very midst.

Nonetheless, as we have said above, some study of the past is helpful, and even necessary, in finding our rightful place in the overall flow of musical development today. Let us then look at the musical eras and styles of the past to better understand our own.

Primitive and ancient music reaches back and down deep into the individual and collective human spirit and psyche, and forms the modal and tonal basis for most primitive religious music found all around the world. It is something basic to all religion, culture, and music of historic humanity. It speaks symbolically of the common origin of our religious longings in the great religions of the world. Out of this came the highly developed and finely balanced Byzantine and Gregorian chants (500–1430) of the Christian faith. Early polyphony, or the use of harmony through the intertwining of related melodies, can be included here and also in the next category. This music can still be alien to Western ears. It uses a multiplicity of more primitive modes and tones that defy the later Western categorization of tonality, and major and minor keys. Some of it sounds dissonant and unexpected in its intervals and melodies. Nonetheless, this music evokes something very deep and mystical in the human spirit in union with the Spirit of God. This is very similar to the spirituality, theology, and ecclesiology found in the writings of the early Church fathers, or Patristics. Many would say that this earlier expression of the Catholic and Orthodox Christian faith is actually far more developed in organizational function, theological thought, and implicit mysticism, than the later more explicit developments. Through the exact and explicit precision of the human mind in later times we sometimes lost the implied intuitive mysticism of the mind of spirit and soul in the earliest expressions of our faith.

The music of the Renaissance (1400–1600), Baroque (1600–1750), and Classical (1750-1820), periods represent a music that developed into something highly mathematical and cerebral in its perception and expression of God and the cosmos. As stated above, this is not so true of the earliest polyphony. The use of formal harmonies of root, third, fifth, seventh and so on, and the categorization into major and minor keys was a great advance in many ways, but we also lost something of the more primal mystery of tone through such usages. The Renaissance would be represented by the music of Josquin, Ockeghem, and Palestrina. Bach, Handel, and Vivaldi represent the Baroque. Spiritually this would be illustrated by the scholastic period of theology and mysticism. But this overemphasis on a mathematically perfect concept of God, the universe, and art overlooked the human heart and the heart of God, and was soon corrected and even overly compensated for in Romanticism.

The Romantic period (1803-1900) is an attempt to rediscover the human heart in music. The music of Beethoven, Borodin, Tchaikovsky, Bruchner, Mahler, and Wagner represent it. In the positive, it symbolizes a rediscovery of the human heart and the mystery of love. Negatively, it represents an almost sickeningly sweet approach to the reality of love. Spiritually this would be illustrated by a devotionalism stuck in superficial emotion, and devoid of the deeper intuitive mysteries of God beyond sense, emotions, or the mind.

Impressionism (1890-1920) is a musical attempt to reflect the non-mathematical aspects of nature, such as crooked lines and squiggles, or ripples proceeding outward from a splash in the water that never resolve back to the source. It is represented by the music of Debussy,

Ravel, Respighi, and Fauré. It employs the use of dis-
sonance in progressions that are actually quite pleas-
ing to the ear, and create a feeling of calm and peace,
like sitting by a lake on a warm spring day, rather than
evoking their usual unsettling effects when played as
clashing notes together. Playing them in progression,
or in the midst of a calming chord, rather than at once
in a way that is isolated and exposed, accomplishes
this. Spiritually this represents the times in our life
when some things just do not seem to make sense in
and of themselves, yet we know that God is still in control. When we are aware of this we actually experience
an almost surreal or supernatural peace and calm in
the midst of the normal conflicts and crises of life. We
sail peacefully and steadfastly on, as in a boat over a
lake filled with non-resolving ripples and waves. All is
well.

Minimalism is a contemporary musical expression
of our own day. It is represented by the music of
Stephen Reich, John Adams, and Philip Glass. Unlike
its graphic art counterpart, musical minimalism uses a
rapid repetition of notes, and short interval and melody
loops, with underlying and undulating chordal masses
moving underneath. It is like the lines coming toward
us on the highway when we are driving down a slowly
curving highway at fast speeds. If we concentrate on
lines we become agitated and nervous. If we look to the
whole experience we are able to be calm and relaxed,
gracefully ease through the curves, and actually find

driving pleasurable and therapeutically soothing. Instead of creating stress, it can actually relieve it! Spiritually, this means learning how to go through the fast-paced experiences of life with a peace and calm that comes from rising above the particular experience and seeing the slower movement of the whole. It means seeing God's greater purpose in even small things of life.

I should also mention Meditational, or Ambient music. This is sometimes called "New Age" music, though those who create it do not necessarily buy into that particular theology. Meditational music is able to hear not only the note, but also the space between the notes. Furthermore, it is able to hear not only the note, but also the space within the note. The sound becomes multidimensional. Silence is as important to the music as is sound itself, leading us on to the Eternal Sound. Furthermore, behind every note the musician must be able to play ten or a hundred notes with near virtuoso skill. Otherwise, there is no authority in the silence. It becomes only silence due to lack of ability. Silence must be a choice not a limitation. Spiritually, this is like hearing silence in, and within, the word proclaimed in a pulpit or read on a page, in order to spiritually perceive the Word. It is the balance of silence and speech, silence in speech, and speech in silence. It proclaims in silence and finds greater authority in speech. It is greater than the written word. It is the mystery of the Eternal and Incarnate Word of God.

The above eras and styles and the spirituality, mysticism, and theology represented by them, must be studied with a relaxed and moderate discipline. Excesses are not needed or helpful. Those who study too much without enjoying the joy of music ministry are like a bow strung too tightly for too long a time. Sooner or later the string will snap, or the bow will break. From time to time the tension from the string must be released. Likewise in our spiritual life. Yes, we must seriously study the things of the Church, doctrine, sacraments, and mysticism, but too much study without recreation, or the deep relaxation of peaceful meditation, can be counterproductive to the spiritual goal we desire. So our discipline should be serious, but moderate, and not excessive. We should take time to relax the strain on the bow of our spiritual life. We should take time for recreation. We should take time for real meditation and prayer that bring great peace, love, and joy.

The Symphony Orchestra

The Symphony Orchestra has often been used as an image of the Church. I have heard this image used many times in homilies, sermons, and teachings in the Catholic Church. The Eastern Orthodox Church would also use the Symphony as an image of the harmony known on earth between the Church and civil authority, or the Christian Empire. This is sometimes called the "Byzantine synthesis." After many historic disappointments in this area, we Catholics have grown to have a more skeptical view of such use of civil authority, though it remains a theoretical possibility. Either way, the Symphony Orchestra is seen as a model of the unity and diversity within the Church.

The symphony orchestra of the Church is based on the humility and love of God Himself within the Trinity. God is One. But God is also goodness and love. Goodness is "self diffusive," therefore; it must have "another" to be good to in order to be realized. But God is also Transcendent, or totally self-sufficient within Himself. Thus a plurality of "persons," or "personas," (as in the "masks" or "personas" of early theatre) within the Oneness of God is required. This is implied in the Elohist tradition of creation in Genesis where God said, "let us make man in our image." By definition love is the selfless union of two from which at least a third is created. Some would say that these are fulfilled by God's creation. But good theology says clearly that creation is a "free" act of God. If God "has" to create, then He is no longer "transcendent" or "wholly other" but is dependent upon creation. Then God is no longer "God" but only a god. God must fulfill his transcendence, goodness, and love, all in one Being. Thus, goodness implies plurality, and love implies Trinity of persons within the Oneness of God. So our Trinitarian God Himself becomes the example for unity and diversity in community in creation. This is the perfect balance of logic and depth of Mystery in love.

The Symphony Orchestra stands in contrast to the rampant individualism of the West, where everyone wants to play the solo. It also stands in contrast to the consumerism of the West, where everyone wants to possess everything for oneself. The Symphony Orchestra says that we all play our part together. There will be times for solos, but that will not be all of the time. Furthermore, by joining together as one, we all possess more than we ever could achieve as isolated individuals. This is a great mystery of unity and diversity. It is also the great Mystery of love. The rich and poor, the weak and strong, join together so that no one who wants to come along is left out or left behind. No one is left in poverty or need, but each has what one needs. Furthermore, because God is a God of abundance, everyone can now enjoy the legitimate and wholesome pleasures of indulging few wants. Yet, we are no longer addicted to our wants as if they are needs. All functions in love and in truth because we have learned how to function together in the Church.

Yet there are still "auditions" for this Symphony Orchestra. As scripture says, "many are called, few are chosen." There are some basic skills necessary to be a part of the Symphony. You must truly love music enough to give your life in the serious pursuit of its beauty. In the Church you must love God through Jesus. But if you really love Him you will be freely willing to lay down your whole life to follow Him. Furthermore, not everyone is called to play every instrument. Most of us are called to specialize in one, or at most just a few. Tryouts help us to discover that to which we are truly called. They are tools for good discernment. In the Church this is not unlike the catechumenate, or the RCIA (Rite of Christian Initiation of Adults), program, where one studies the basics to discern whether or not to become a Roman Catholic. It is also similar to entering into a Postulancy or "time for questioning," or a Novitiate or "new membership," of a religious or monastic community within the Church. If one is serious about membership we will freely do the work to meet the minimal requirements out of love, not as drudgery, or out of constraint.

Within the Symphony Orchestra there are sections of various kinds of instruments. There is a string section, subdivided into the violin, viola, cello, and double bass sections. Likewise there is a brass section for the trumpets, trombones, French horns, tubas and so on. There's also the woodwind section for flute, clarinet, oboe, English horn, and bassoon, etc., and a percussion section for the various kinds of drums, cymbals, and other world instruments. These sections are like the various communities and movements raised by the Spirit throughout the history of the Church. Each section has its own leader and character, yet it exists within the greater whole of the Symphony Orchestra.

There's also a musical score and sheet music for the Symphony Orchestra. Though there are often many notes appearing at one time, each instrument can only play one, or a few, out of the greater chord. Each player must have a sense of the whole sound and direction in order to play their part well, but they cannot play everything at once. It is not enough to play the notes on the page. One must have a sense of the spirit, or intention, of the composer as directed by the conductor. Otherwise, it just remains a lifeless technical performance. Likewise with liturgy, each person must do their part with a sense of the greater unity and good of the whole. It is not enough to technically recite the responses of clergy, laity, or the various ministries of music, lector, and so forth. We must truly understand the spirit behind the actions and words of liturgy. Otherwise, the liturgy remains a vain or fruitless ritual.

Related to this is the sacramental, or mysterious, aspect of the Symphony Orchestra. The spirit of the composer of the music must be truly present when played, or else it is not considered a good performance. This occurs when all the players, section leaders, and conductor, freely cooperate with the known intention of the composer for the symphonic work. The same is true in liturgy. It is sacramental, especially in liturgies associated with the direct celebration of the sacraments. In a most special way the Spirit of God is present in the sacraments. In an extraordinary way Jesus himself is truly present within the Eucharist under the appearance of bread and wine, even as his divinity from God the Father and the Spirit was present under the appearance of humanity born of the Virgin Mary. Jesus was fully human and fully divine, yet without sinning or losing touch with fallen humanity. This is a great Mystery beyond human comprehension, yet believed by faith as divine revelation from God for Jesus. This leads humanity to share in His divinity, even as He shared in our humanity. This too is Mystery.

A conductor directs the entire Symphony Orchestra. Without a conductor the orchestra will fall into chaos as each interprets the score for themselves. The conductor brings order, peace, and direction to the orchestra. The conductor must intimately know the workings of the entire orchestra. He must know the instruments and how they work best. He must also know the players as people on a professionally personal level. He must also know both the spirit and the musical scores of the various composers and their respective works. Yet, he cannot play the instruments himself. He cannot control the people who play them as if they were robots or puppets. To the contrary, it is his job to call forth, to inspire, and to point the way. It is up to the Symphony Orchestra itself to go there.

Likewise, in the Church, Jesus is the ultimate Conductor. There are various section leaders within the Symphony Orchestra of the Church, and behind-the-scenes administrators who help it to function well. Furthermore, in his bodily absence between his

Ascension and Second Coming, there are pastors who shepherd the flock of the Church in his place. This happens on an international, regional, and local level. Within Roman Catholicism we see this very clearly in the Pope and the bishops of the various dioceses who succeed Peter and the Apostles, and in the pastor of the local parish church.

As we have said, there are also other leaders within the Symphony Orchestra. There are section leaders in the Orchestra itself. There are also workers behind the scenes in the administrative offices and so on. Likewise in the Church there are auxiliary bishops, associate pastors, as well as those who work in the ministries of administration, healing, teaching, and so on, that are not always visible in a liturgical celebration of the whole community.

But there are other configurations within the Symphony Orchestra that make it all the more interesting. There is the Chamber Orchestra, the Ensemble, Jazz Group, the Rock Group, the Folk Group, soloists, and the various new integrations of all of the above. The Church is a "community of communities."

The Chamber Orchestra is a smaller version of the full Symphony Orchestra. It is usually used for accompaniment for solo pieces for guitar, violin, cello and the like. Though smaller, it still functions under the same general principles as the full symphony orchestra. It has a conductor, has sections and section leaders, and plays music from a written score.

Spiritually, this is like the various monastic and consecrated communities within the overall Church. Monasticism, in particular, is called a "quasi Church," for it is a microcosm of the Church. At the height of the medieval Church, the abbot of a monastery was, more or less, on equal footing with the bishops. Even today, the abbot and major superiors of other monastic and consecrated communities have "ordinary" power over the monks and the brothers and sisters of their respective communities.

The Ensemble is also a smaller configuration that usually plays more formal pieces of music. However, while the Ensemble has a leader, they are usually one of the players, and do not stand before the group to conduct. Furthermore, some of the more modern music for Ensembles allows ample time for improvisation, or playing without specific notes on a page. This symbolizes some of the less formal movements of the Church like Marriage Encounter and Cursillo. On an ecumenical level, it is similar to churches such as the Methodist, Baptist, or other Evangelical expressions.

Next comes the Jazz Group. This is a group of very accomplished musicians capable of playing with virtuosity in almost any style. Like the Ensemble, the Jazz Group also has a leader among the players, but most of the notes performed are improvisational, with only minimal direction in the sheet music. This style of music takes great virtuosity on one's instrument, great training from the past, and great confidence in the present.

In the Church this is very similar to the Charismatic and Pentecostal expressions of faith. These expressions are open to Church and community leadership and the direction of good theology and doctrine, but they are most open to the spontaneous working of the Holy Spirit in the individual believer's life and in the life of the charismatic community. This takes great discernment and accomplishment in the things of the Spirit on the part of the individual and community.

The Rock/Pop Group is very similar to the Jazz Group in makeup, but the style is significantly different. Though often quite advanced, the style is more simple and less technically accomplished, so it can be played by musicians who are less formally trained, and to better represent the average person. The sound is really too diverse to characterize in one particular style, but ranges all the way from Hard Rock, to R & B, to Rap. Nowadays, it can even include new Country! What is important in the music is its attitude in the message, and in some cases, its actual message. Many rock songs have become "themes" for modern popular culture at a given time. It is often a prophetic, and even a caustic, musical representation of the culture in which we live. This can be both positive and negative. Sometimes these artists move to the margins of music after a few years, but they never totally leave because they love music too much.

In the Church this symbolizes the ministry of the prophet. The prophet is usually not very popular in the institutional mainstream, but is supported among the marginal. Because of this, they may have to suffer greatly, even in the midst of their popular support. Yet, the true prophet does not leave the Church. They love it too deeply. Rather, they stay and bear the consequences of their actions in obedience to those in authority. Time tests the authenticity of their message.

The Folk Group is similar. Actually, many have said that Pop Music in general, including Rock and Country, is really the folk music of our time. I would agree. As my brother Terry says in concert, "folk singers sing songs that folks can sing!" It is the music of the people. Ironically, many of the great symphonies of classical music are based on the simple folk melodies of a given region. It has an ability to represent and stir up the spirit of the people. In the Church there are also ministries that represent and stir up the work of the Holy Spirit in the people. Leaders in the Church learned to listen to, what St. John Henry Newman called, "the sense of the faithful."

Within all of the groups mentioned above there is also room for the soloist. From symphonic orchestral pieces to folk music there's always the space provided for solos by various instruments and singers. During the solo the individual is able to show their particular skill at singing or playing. Often, they have extraordinary skill and virtuosity that is able to communicate the spirit of the composition in the most moving way. Sometimes, because of the unavailability of qualified people to make up the Symphony Orchestra, Chamber Group, Ensemble, Jazz, Rock, or Folk group, the soloist must play entirely on their own. But, even then, the soloist finds their identity, and resulting authority, within the overall community of past and present musicians on a local, regional, national, and international level. The support and identity of other musicians on this universal level is always important for the sense of authority even for the soloist.

In the Church this applies to the ministries of the evangelist or prophet. They may minister during formal liturgy, or in extraordinary gatherings outside of liturgy within the church building, or outside in the world. In the most particular way it applies to the vocation of the Christian hermit, and the balance between solitude and community in their call. They may live in hermitage deep in the wilderness or faraway in the desert, but they are always part of the greater community of the Church. Specifically, hermits have usually organized into "colonies," or "communities," whereby individual hermit "cells" (or the place where heaven, as in "celestial" comes to earth) are scattered around common buildings and a central church or chapel. These hermit communities come together for common liturgy, meals, and meetings and fellowship, on a daily, or weekly basis. The ministry of Evangelist and Prophet, as well as the vocation of the hermit is on the rise within the Church today. Lastly, it applies to the cantor in sacred music itself. They may sometimes function alone, but they always see themselves, first, as part of the greater congregation of the Church, and second, as part of and complement to a choir whenever possible.

Perhaps the most exciting development in music today is the new integration of all of the above in a single performance of the Symphony Orchestra. The integration of these and other styles and configurations manifests the past in the present as we point towards the future of music. This is exciting! Spiritually we see this happening in the new movements and communities raised up by the Spirit in the Church, the theological explanation of them, and the canonical and structural accommodation for them in the overall life of the Church. It is also happening in sacred music itself. This manifestation of new integrations is nothing less than continuing the building of the spiritual temple of the Church which is built squarely upon the spiritual stones of those who have come before. Year after year, layer upon layer of spiritual stones is laid into the temple of the Church. This goes all the way back to the foundation of the apostles and prophets with Christ Jesus as the cornerstone. As with music, this is most exciting to be a part of today!

To conclude, it is important to remember the difference between the rehearsal and the concert. Rehearsal is most important, especially the dress rehearsal. But even the dress rehearsal is not the concert. There are still corrections to be made. Mistakes are sometimes made. That is what the dress rehearsal is for! It's like the difference between "run throughs" and "takes" in recording. The difference between a "run through" and a "take" is significant. When the engineer hits the record button in the studio, the seriousness and hopefully the quality of the playing goes up significantly. The energy, and sometimes the stress levels, in the performance rise. Furthermore it's like the difference between basic "takes" and "overdubs" in finishing the work. Even though a basic take has been recorded, the group or the individual has the opportunity to go back and to "punch in" and out of particular sections of the music in order to fix mistakes, or give a more moving performance. This is a common practice in both classical and popular recording today. Spiritually, this means that our life in the Church is a rehearsal for heaven. Mistakes can and will be made. That's why we have the sacrament of Penance! So we should not be too uptight about being perfect, though we should strive to do our best as a response to the grace of God. The Lord calls us to perfection. But perfectionism actually keeps us from reaching the goal.

Lastly, the spiritual music of the Master Musician is always seen as just a doorway to the Infinite. It is not infinite. People often tell me that my music is prayer. But I respond and say, rather, that it is a doorway to prayer. It is a tool of God, not God. It is meant to guide people to God, but not meant to, even subtly, be turned into a false god or idol. The Music of God is really best heard in silence. Earthly music leads to the place where we can hear that which is beyond the hearing of the ear. It is Music of universal essence and spirit that permeates all the energies of body, soul, and all creation. It can be hinted to by the music of this earth, but it can never totally contain or express it. It must be heard in silence, but if heard there, it can be heard everywhere and in all things.

In the end Jesus is the Master Musician, the Composer, and the Conductor of this Divine Music of God. The Church is the Symphony Orchestra with all of its integrations of style and configuration. The Pope conducts as we sojourn on the face of this earth. The bishops, priests, deacons, and various lay ministers are the leaders of the various sections, and behind-the-scenes administrators of this great Symphony Orchestra. The liturgy is the score. The Spirit of the Composer is just waiting to be unlocked in every note and word.

We must learn to make God's Music. It is up to us to use the instrument of our life within the Symphony Orchestra of the Church. It is up to us to individually respond, yet to join together to play and sing. It is up to us to make the Music of God. So come, the Master calls. The others are assembling. The Music is waiting to be played.

Additional Titles Published by Resurrection Press, a Catholic Book Publishing Imprint

A Rachel Rosary *Larry Kupferman*	$4.50
Blessings All Around *Dolores Leckey*	$8.95
Catholic Is Wonderful *Mitch Finley*	$4.95
Come, Celebrate Jesus! *Francis X. Gaeta*	$4.95
Days of Intense Emotion *Keeler/Moses*	$12.95
From Holy Hour to Happy Hour *Francis X. Gaeta*	$7.95
Healing through the Mass *Robert DeGrandis, SSJ*	$9.95
The Healing Rosary *Mike D.*	$5.95
Healing Your Grief *Ruthann Williams, OP*	$7.95
Healthy and Holy Under Stress *Muto, VanKaam*	$3.95
Heart Peace *Adolfo Quezada*	$9.95
Life, Love and Laughter *Jim Vlaun*	$7.95
Living Each Day by the Power of Faith *Barbara Ryan*	$8.95
The Joy of Being a Catechist *Gloria Durka*	$4.95
The Joy of Being a Eucharistic Minister *Mitch Finley*	$5.95
The Joy of Marriage Preparation *McDonough*	$5.95
The Joy of Preaching *Rod Damico*	$6.95
The Joy of Ushers *Gretchen Hailer*	$5.95
Lights in the Darkness *Ave Clark, O.P.*	$8.95
Loving Yourself for God's Sake *Adolfo Quezada*	$5.95
Mother Teresa *Eugene Palumbo*	$5.95
Our Grounds for Hope *Fulton J. Sheen*	$7.95
Personally Speaking *Jim Lisante*	$8.95
Practicing the Prayer of Presence *van Kaam/Muto*	$8.95
5-Minute Miracles *Linda Schubert*	$4.95
Season of New Beginnings *Mitch Finley*	$4.95
Season of Promises *Mitch Finley*	$4.95
Stay with Us *John Mullin, SJ*	$3.95
Surprising Mary *Mitch Finley*	$7.95
What He Did for Love *Francis X. Gaeta*	$5.95
You Are My Beloved *Mitch Finley*	$10.95
Your Sacred Story *Robert Lauder*	$6.95

For a free catalog call 1-800-892-6657